HRH THE PRINCE OF WALES

A VISION OF BRITAIN

A PERSONAL VIEW OF ARCHITECTURE

Doubleday

LONDON · NEW YORK · TORONTO · SYDNEY · AUCKLAND

DOUBLEDAY, a division of Transworld Publishers Ltd
61–63 Uxbridge Road, London W5 5SA

DOUBLEDAY, a division of Bantam Doubleday Dell Publishing Group, Inc
666 Fifth Avenue, New York, New York 10103

DOUBLEDAY CANADA LTD
105 Bond Street, Toronto, Ontario

TRANSWORLD PUBLISHERS (AUSTRALIA) PTY LTD
15–23 Helles Avenue, Moorebank, NSW 2170

TRANSWORLD PUBLISHERS (NZ) LTD
Cnr Moselle and Waipareira Aves, Henderson, Auckland

First published 1989
Copyright © A.G. Carrick Ltd, 1989

Designed by Associated Design Consultants Ltd, London
Typeset by Lazy Dog, London
Reproduction by Alpha Reprographics Ltd, London
Printed in West Germany by Mohndruck Graphische Betriebe GmbH, Gütersloh

British Library Cataloguing in Publication Data

Charles, *Prince of Wales, 1948–*
A Vision of Britain: A Personal View of Architecture
1. Great Britain. Buildings. Architectural features
I. Title
720′.941

United States Library of Congress Cataloging-in-Publication Data

Charles, *Prince of Wales, 1948–*
A Vision of Britain
Includes index
1. Charles, *Prince of Wales, 1948–* – Contributions in architecture 2. Architecture – Great Britain
3. Architecture, Modern – 20th century – Great Britain 4. Architecture and society – Great Britain
5. Architecture – Great Britain – Human factors
I. Title
NA968.C48 1989   720′.941   89-1527
ISBN 0-385-26903-X

HRH THE PRINCE OF WALES

A VISION OF BRITAIN

A PERSONAL VIEW OF ARCHITECTURE

This book is dedicated to my grandmother,
who always encouraged me to look and to observe

CONTENTS

Introduction

6

A Vision of Britain

16

Ten Principles

75

Conclusion

154

Acknowledgements

158

Index

159

I must confess to the reader right from the start my hesitation in putting pen to paper. It is not out of fear of venturing, yet again, into a territory positively bristling with porcupine-like professionals and cantankerous critics – although I humbly acknowledge my lack of academic credentials for the expedition. No, it is because I feel I would write so much more sense if I waited until I was very old and, hopefully, correspondingly wise. Such hesitation, of course, is pointless. First of all I would probably fail to reach old age and a state of wisdom, having been felled in the prime of life by a piece of rotting concrete descending from a post-modernist building and, secondly, I recall the old adage that 'he who hesitates is lost'.

Before I go any further I would just like to emphasise that my particular interest in architecture and the environment is not a result of my trying to find something to fill my day and then settling on this subject. For a long time I have felt strongly about the wanton destruction which has taken place in this country in the name of progress; about the sheer, unadulterated ugliness and mediocrity of public and commercial buildings, and of housing estates, not to mention the dreariness and heartlessness of so much urban planning. At the time I was far too young to do anything about it, but I remember thinking in the 1960s how crazy it was to destroy so much of value and, by obeying the dictates of fashion, to throw the baby out with the bathwater. This frenzied attack on long-established principles and values affected not only architecture, but also music, art and education.

The fashionable architectural theories of the 50s and 60s, so slavishly followed by those who wanted to be considered 'with it', have spawned deformed monsters which have come to haunt our towns and cities, our villages and our countryside. As a result of thirty years of experimenting with revolutionary building materials and

Above: Many of us develop attachments, sometimes without realising it, to particularly familiar and distinguished buildings like the National Gallery in London, of which I am a Trustee. When, in 1984, I said in a speech to the RIBA that the proposed extension to the Gallery was like a 'monstrous carbuncle on the face of a much-loved and elegant friend', it was meant merely as a personal observation. Only after I said it did I begin to appreciate from the response just how many people felt as I did.

After my film was broadcast the BBC's 'Daytime Live' invited viewers to send in pictures of buildings which they felt had ruined the towns that they lived in. Hundreds of people responded, and the BBC decided to exhibit the pictures, with their comments. The Building Centre refused to exhibit them, and Building News called the exhibition a 'smelly little show' when it finally did find a venue. I am happy to show some of the 'carbuncles' here. Top right: The Link Centre, Swindon, Wiltshire: 'I was convinced that the appendages were scaffolding' (Ron Gosney). Right: Visitors' Centre, Conisbrough Castle, South Yorkshire: 'The Centre has rooms that are supposed to represent "Medieval Tents"' (Mr and Mrs J.E. Bowen). Lower right: Post Office Sorting Office, Putney, London: 'This "Lego" building is in a Conservation Area. The neighbourhood awoke one morning to find a bright blue steel roof being put on. We could not believe our eyes' (Mrs Robin Barber). Bottom right: DIY store, Eastbourne, Sussex: 'Imagine living opposite a view like this? It dominates this row of cottages' (Mrs S. Hind-March). Centre right: Belfast City Hospital: 'It replaced a beautiful old stone building, which can be seen in the background. I realise that the old hospital was small and cramped, but why did the new one have to look like this?' (Paula McCaughey).

Top right: Tricorn Centre, Portsmouth: 'Someone round here once called it "mildewed elephant droppings covered in drainpipes"' (Catherine Gladdis). Right: Victoria Flats, Nottingham: 'It was at one time the Victoria Railway Station and was a beautiful old building. Even the architects must have had pangs of guilt, for they left the original tower of the station' (Mrs M. Smith).

novel ideas, burning all the rule books and purveying the theory that man is a machine, we have ended up with Frankenstein monsters, devoid of character, alien and largely unloved, except by the professors who have been concocting these horrors in their laboratories – and even they find their creations a bit hard to take after a while. The rest of us are constantly obliged to endure the results of their experiments and, judging by the reactions to *A Vision of Britain*, the film I made with the BBC, very few people are pleased with the situation.

Out of nearly 5,000 letters I received after the film, 99% agreed with my feelings on this subject. 0.5% were qualified in their approval of the points I was trying to make. Various suggestions were made by all sorts of people about how the situation might be improved. One of the most common was that children *must* receive some form of architectural or environmental education in schools. The other was that the powers of the Department of the Environment and local authorities should be better regulated in the interests of individuals, and not of property developers. I was also interested and heartened to see the overwhelming

degree of editorial support throughout the media for many of the views I expressed in the BBC film.

Some people like to portray my views on architecture and the environment as thoroughly reactionary and opposed to progress and the requirements of the contemporary world. The further I delve into the shadowy world of architecture, planning and property development the more I become aware of the powerful influence of various interest groups. Hence the frequently violent and vitriolic reactions to the points I have been making. I am condemned for entering complicated and dangerous waters where even the most sophisticated professional might founder. I am even accused of abusing my power (sic) as Prince of Wales by intervening in matters best left to the architectural profession and, can you believe it, of acting undemocratically.

I am told that I am being grossly unfair to the architectural profession by levelling my fire at architects when, in fact, it was the planners, the developers, the local and national politicians who were really to blame. Why then, *have* I been levelling my fire at *architects*, in particular? It is because I believe

that it *was* the architectural establishment, or a powerful group within it, which made the running in the 50s and 60s. It was they who set the cultural agenda. They were extremely persuasive and they were very successful in their demonstration of the requirement for a 'new' architecture that would meet the need for rebuilding post-war Britain.

It wasn't the local councillors, or the developers, who had read Le Corbusier and other apostles of modernism, and then persuaded reluctant architects to adopt 'progressive' ideas. Architects deliberately staged a revolution within their own organisation and their own system of education. It was the 'great architects' of this period who convinced everyone that the world would be safe in their hands. Their descendants still retain prestige, and a kind of glamour, among their peers: they set the style, control the curriculum, and have commanding positions in the Royal Institute of British Architects, the Royal Fine Art Commission, and the Royal Academy. It is they who keep a tight grip on architectural education and who are the heroes of a largely sycophantic architectural press, and the focus of much uncritical attention from the media in general. Indeed these people are so used to escaping criticism that my mild observation that the design for No 1 Poultry looked 'like an old 1930s wireless', was treated in some quarters as an unconstitutional interference in the planning process.

It may sound facile to say so, but I don't particularly want to have to battle with architects, or developers for that matter.

However, their philosophical approach to the whole question of the design of the built environment as it affects people and the lives they live, is what concerns me. Many architects and developers believe that architecture should reflect the

Below: Earl's Way, Runcorn. People condemned to live out their lives in a grubby launderette.

spirit of the age – whatever that might be! In the same way that the Renaissance reflected in its architecture the throwing-off of the shackles of the medieval church, so, these people maintain, today's architecture must reflect the dominance of high technology and man's apparent mechanical triumph over nature which, for so long, held him in thrall. The past, apparently, is largely irrelevant in this scheme of things, and its meaning and lessons must be obliterated.

I believe that when a man loses contact with the past he loses his soul. Likewise, if we deny the architectural past – and the lessons to be learnt from our ancestors – then our buildings also lose *their* souls. If we abandon the traditional *principles* upon which architecture was based for 2,500 years or more, then our civilisation suffers. Our lives may be dominated by contemporary forms of sophisticated technology, but we are also the heirs of something far greater. Deep down in our subconscious an uneasy feeling persists that there is something missing if we sacrifice ourselves on the altar of progress, and live and work in buildings which only reflect the technology of the moment.

There is nothing wrong in learning from the past; in applying the lessons our forebears learnt so painfully; in recognising that our own particular island heritage came about as a result of a response to climatic conditions, the availability of certain local materials, and through the inspiration of the grander examples of European architecture. These features give us a sense of belonging and a sense of order, which are vital to our development as human beings. We are not the only ones to feel anxious about the course that modernist, or even post-modernist architecture, is taking. (And don't be confused by post-modernism, and all the other 'isms' that clever architectural critics and commentators conjure up in order to lull us into a false sense of security!)

In countries such as Saudi Arabia, where the pace of development has been astonishingly rapid, and where the prevailing feeling used to be that, 'if it's American and if it is in "the international style" it must be the best thing for us,' they are now beginning to realise that they have lost something in the rush to modernise along Western lines. A movement is developing which seeks to rediscover the Islamic and indigenous heritage, and to learn from the local environmental wisdom of ancestors who knew so well how to build appropriately for the prevailing climatic conditions.

People in the Middle East are now listening with increasing interest to a remarkable Egyptian architect called Dr Hassan Fathy who, for forty years, has had to put up with persistent vitriolic criticism and denigration by the modernist architectural establishment because he continued to espouse the cause of traditional Islamic architecture. He was dismissed as a romantic and out of touch with modern reality. 'When you remind people of aesthetics and culture,' Dr Fathy wrote, 'they say you are romantic. This shows the state of our society today.' He was criticised, as James Steele has written in his fascinating monograph on Fathy, for being an 'artist-architect', by which they mean, I take it, that he's altogether too interested in aesthetics, and altogether not interested enough in all those seductive possibilities that now supposedly exist for the architect to bring about social change and the general betterment of mankind, through technology and political pressure.

Dr Fathy believes that 'architecture for the poor should not be approached like a treatment for a special disease.' He advocates an 'architecture that can be used by rich and poor alike', not one that is the privilege of a particular class of people. Aesthetics should be a consideration in *all* architecture:

'*Unfortunately,*' Fathy claims, '*the poor are not now given the advantage of aesthetics. People wrongly associate poverty with ugliness, which is a mistake. The less expensive, the poorer the project, the more care and attention that should be paid to aesthetics.*' (My italics.)

Dr Fathy is a remarkable man whose courageous voice deserves to be heard. Just listen to this: 'I say that beautiful architecture is an act of civility towards the person who comes into the building. It bows to you at every corner, as in a minuet…

Every ugly or senseless building is an insult to the man passing in front of it. Every building should be embellishing and adding to its culture. *This is very difficult to do now because we have abandoned human scale and "human reference". We need to reintroduce human scale, human reference and musicality in architecture.*' (My italics.)

Because of the desire to abandon the past as an irrelevance, so much of priceless value has been lost or destroyed. 'The revealed knowledge of the sage,' Fathy says, 'is now replaced by modern analytical science, while the skill of the craftsman's hand has been replaced by the machine.'

It is encouraging therefore to learn that one of Dr Fathy's most gifted pupils, Abdel Wahed El-Wakil, is working in Britain, and that through his work with traditional materials and forms of decoration he is trying to heal what he calls the 'destructive division' between artists, craftsmen, and architects. I hope his considerable skills can be put to use here.

The point I am trying to make is that there is a profound unease – not only in Britain, but also throughout Europe, the Middle East and, to a certain extent, in North America

Right: I admire the perfection of Islamic architecture in the Taj Mahal, India.

Above: El-Wakil's house at Hydra, in Greece and (left) mosque on the Jeddah Corniche. He regards himself as not so much an 'Islamic', more a 'traditional' architect.

– about the architectural course which has been adopted and which until recently people have felt powerless to influence.

In a rapidly changing world, with new technological breakthroughs every other day, what on earth is wrong with people desiring surroundings which are familiar, traditional, well-tried and beautiful? Such a desire does not mean that we are any the less 'modern'; that we are suddenly going to revert to a pre-industrial existence and behave in an 18th-century fashion. Far from it. It seems to me that such a union of apparent opposites is essential for our sanity in today's world. What is so badly needed is for the architects, and the developers who employ them, to be more sensitive to the deep-rooted feelings of 'ordinary' people and to find ways of integrating their opinions and their needs into the creative processes from which new buildings emerge.

Most planners, I am happy to see, are becoming more sympathetic to these ideas, and would like architects to involve the public more. Only in this way are we likely to be able to make our inner cities (*and* the peripheral housing estates for that matter) more civilised, more intimate, more habitable and more

friendly. At present I firmly believe that many of the mistakes of the past are in danger of being made again because a substantial proportion of the people responsible for new developments are still anchored to the ideas and sacred cows of the 60s.

There is a new breed of younger architects, however, whose inspiration stems from the hard-won wisdom of their forebears, but they are derided by the dominant modernist establishment. Any hope of a true renaissance in design and building techniques, which can be harnessed to the rebuilding of Britain, is unlikely to succeed unless the pattern of education in architectural schools throughout the United Kingdom is radically overhauled. At present to my knowledge there is no school where architectural design is taught on traditional lines. Students who show a desire to learn such principles are often actively discouraged. As a consequence, they emerge from architectural school in a kind of 'designer vacuum'. At the feet of their teachers they have learnt, like parrots, to cry 'pastiche' at any fellow architect rash enough to attempt to design buildings along traditional lines.

Yet they themselves have merely learnt to ape the superficial mannerisms of the fashionable architects of the day, not the underlying principles of composition. But now there is, I suspect, a mounting desire on the part of potential young architects to learn the true and ancient *art* of architecture – the hard way, by sheer application and effort – even though they are frustrated at every turn. This arrogant attitude on the part of architectural schools really does have to be challenged if we are to see any progress. Tradition need not rule out progress.

There is no doubt, of course, that the mood has begun to change in the last few years. G.K. Chesterton once wrote, 'We are the people of England, that never have spoken yet.' Well, the people of Britain *have* now begun to speak about what kind of architecture they want.

The community architecture movement, for instance, has steadily transformed the lives of what must

by now be thousands of people who have taken an active role in the building of their own homes, the shaping of their own communities, and the creation of more congenial urban surroundings. As a consequence encouragingly large areas of towns and cities have been transformed, and released from blight and decay. This has been achieved by soliciting the views of the residents, rather than ignoring them. It really is extraordinary what can be done by quite simple means.

In Newcastle I looked at a small-scale scheme – much more modest than the vast Urban Development Corporation project a mile or so away – where they have quietly adapted a theatre and arts centre in a street of terraced houses which, I'm happy to say, still has a village-like quality. They haven't really altered the basic appearance of the area because they have respected the original character of the surroundings. As a result it is working. Commercial investment is flowing in, and the whole area is being transformed. There is a mood of confidence and hope in the future.

There are encouraging things like this happening all over the country, but they tend to be rather isolated achievements. In my film I

asked whether we couldn't organise things on a more fundamental level so that improvement could be more widespread. The response by the public and the press to my proposal that we ought to consider the adoption of a kind of code based on ten principles or suggestions encouraged me to reflect more carefully on the question of writing down a few generally agreed rules – if you can ever reach such a thing as general agreement! Later in the book I try to spell out in more detail what I mean by these 'ten principles' or 'ten commandments' although, of course, they aren't commandments at all, but more like pieces of folklore drawn from our inherited experience: rules which we put into practice for centuries without thinking too much about it

Right: When I visited Newcastle I saw proposals for the Newcastle Theatre Village. By respecting the historic fabric and innate quality of this part of the city, new investment should be attracted into it. Above right: Helping to build a better Britain.

Below: Edinburgh's picturesque medieval town overlooks the late-18th-century New Town in which the streets were laid out on a regular pattern, and great care was taken with height, materials and proportion. The result is the most beautiful city in Britain. Top right: Building the Montparnasse Tower in 1973 within the historic fabric of Paris was a mistake which the French did not repeat. More recent urban redevelopment near the Tower respects the old grain of the city. Bottom right: This addition to the courtyard of the Louvre, although controversial, recalls Napoleon's Egyptian conquests in a modern idiom.

and which resulted at one time in Britain having some of the most beautiful towns and cities in the world.

It was illuminating to talk to Andres Duany, the architect of Seaside – the town on the Gulf of Mexico that was shown in the film – because he has developed his theories about a code much further, and his ideas are being viewed with growing interest all over America. His code has already been taken up, not only in some middle-class communities, but also in hard-pressed inner urban areas. It is often forgotten that the idea of a code goes back to the ancient classical world. Codes are part of our civilisation. They operated throughout Europe where Paris, Bologna, Prague, Edinburgh (in my

estimation the most beautiful city in Britain), Vienna and, as I mentioned in the film, Siena were all the result of architects and builders working within an agreed framework.

Such a framework could be used, I believe, to great effect in rebuilding the shattered remnants of our inner cities so that people once again have proper communities in which to live and which, in turn, restore life and soul to such inner urban areas. Through an organisation called Business in the Community, of which I am President, I am hoping we can encourage the development of 'urban villages' in order to reintroduce human scale, intimacy and a vibrant street life. These factors can help to restore to people their sense of belonging and pride in their own particular surroundings.

While in Paris last year, I was much impressed by a visit I made to

a formerly rundown area of the city in Montparnasse. In this case an agreed framework had led to the retention of traditional street patterns on a narrower, more intimate scale, which opened out, at various points, into small squares or piazzas. The height of the buildings was limited and so the retention of human scale was ensured. And it contrasted spectacularly with the vast, impersonal 1960s monoliths, seemingly about to trample, Gulliver-like, on their miniature neighbours. The significant part about this most imaginative and immediately attractive development, as far as any architect anxious that his creative powers might be restricted is concerned, is that within the basic framework of street widths and building heights there is room for a large range of styles. It is the *scale* which counts.

Some additions to Truro over the last twenty years might have been designed by a visitor from another planet. Below: Evans and Shalev's new law courts enrich the skyline of Truro.

Likewise, the French have been clever – and shown great taste – in the scale of the new glass pyramid designed by the Chinese-American architect I.M. Pei in the forecourt of the Louvre. While I am not sure that I would myself have placed such an edifice on that particular spot, it has been designed with great care in order to harmonise as far as possible with the Louvre itself. The colour of the pyramid, its four surrounding smaller pyramids, and the granite borders of the elegant fountains, match the colour of the Louvre, and the proportions are pleasing.

Here in Britain there are increasingly encouraging signs – like the new Courts of Justice in Truro, which happily enhance the skyline of the capital of my Duchy.

But we can't relax; we do need to think hard about our environment. We do need to continue and open up the debate which has started about the sort of Britain we are building. We do need to consider such possibilities as 'codes'. With their use, our towns and cities *can* be restored to places where *people* matter once more and where our spirits find tranquillity and inspiration. We all need *beauty*. We can't live without it – as we've all discovered to our communal cost. We should therefore no longer be nervous about 'aesthetic' questions, and no longer anxious about applying 'aesthetic' judgements. Where we failed to exercise such judgements in the recent past we allowed buildings which are the very opposite of beautiful. But it wasn't inevitable that they should be so. We don't have to let it happen any more.

We *can* build new developments which echo the familiar, attractive features of our regional vernacular styles. There *are* architects who can design with sensitivity and imagination so that people can live in more pleasing surroundings. And not just in our towns and cities. It is possible in country areas, for instance, through the agency of good rural housing associations, to build straightforward, visually appealing houses in local materials for people on lower incomes. I know this from the work of the Sutton (Hastoe) Housing Association, which operates near Sandringham House.

At present, under the existing planning and highway regulations, it is next to impossible to achieve the kind of changes I have been suggesting. The present regulations and requirements seem inevitably to lead to the usual monotonous uniformity of housing developments where every house has to have precisely the same amenities: the same garden size, the same style, the same road width in front of it and so on. The secret, surely, is to accept that each person lays different emphases on his or her requirements, and to see therefore that it *is* possible to create developments which echo the traditional, more intimate, patterns of our villages and towns.

We *can* do better. Our fellow citizens are demanding that we do better. It is up to the developers, the architects, the planners and the politicians to respond.

I would suggest that most of us are probably very proud of our country and feel there is something rather special about Britain, about our landscape, about our villages and our towns, and about those aspects of our surroundings which provide us with what we rather loosely call character. This character, which is so evident in the local architectural styles of the buildings you see in each county, is part of an extraordinarily rich tradition which we've inherited from our forebears.

'An extraordinarily rich tradition...'
of regional building styles and materials

Top left: Lower Slaughter in Gloucestershire. Honey-coloured Cotswold stone, tiled roofs, and the traditional skills of local craftsmen created an ideal of the English village.
Bottom left: Red brick oast houses in Kent.

Above: Crofters' cottages in the Scottish Highlands face out the weather in whitewashed stone and slate.
Top right: A huddle of thatch, tile and stone in Wootton Courtenay, Somerset.
Bottom right: Timber and plaster dominate Chester's High Street.

Above: Whitby's houses of local sandstone and slate slope down to the fishing harbour on the edge of the North Yorkshire moors.

Left: The great railway viaduct at Leaderfoot, Scotland, spans the river Tweed, with the old eighteenth-century stone road bridge in the foreground. This is an example of engineering technology exploiting the materials of the region and enhancing and adding drama to the landscape rather than destroying it.

Above: The Brandon Estate, built in 1960, looms above the traditional terraces of London's Kennington. All over Britain cities were devastated by planners, politicians and architects who sought to build 'cities of towers'. Left: Great cliffs of buildings replaced the old terraced housing which, for all its faults, had been built to human scale and had sustained living communities.

Some time during this century something went wrong. For various complicated reasons, we allowed terrible damage to be inflicted on parts of this country's unique landscape and townscape. Having summoned up my courage to express an opinion on the quality of our surroundings, I have been fascinated to discover on my travels just how many people seem to be appalled by what we have done to so many of our towns and cities since the last war. I can assure you that I wouldn't be saying all this now if I felt that I was alone in having these opinions.

At the moment we are in the middle of another great building boom, so further huge changes to our environment are already in motion. The important question now is whether we can get it right this time, with this second chance.

Above: New or 'neo-vernacular' houses in Skipton. They're designed with respect for the place's past, using local stone, and built in traditional style. And the residents seem to like it.

Left: This grand sweep of magnificent English countryside which I painted in Yorkshire, is part of Wensleydale. Such countryside demands extremely sensitive handling when trying to fit buildings into it.

When I visited Skipton, in North Yorkshire, I was struck by the fact that this market town still keeps the local character of the Dales. Its own identity is still intact and it looks much as it did a hundred years ago. The terraced houses don't appear to have changed much, and they still provide sensible housing.

I visited a housing association development that was built in a part of town that had become derelict. The association's policy is to keep the rents low to encourage people back to the town centre. And they have used local stone and slate to build homes that echo the old terraced houses.

But what, I wanted to know, do people think of their new homes? When I am travelling around the country I try to find out. In Skipton I met Mrs Huck who told me about her new flat. She had some ingenious ideas about using glass furniture to make the place seem larger, and she even had a dual-purpose grandfather clock – it was certainly the first time I had seen one used as a drinks cabinet!

Above: Skipton Building Society. They used stone, but why try to dominate the skyline like this? You'd think a building society would have more respect for the scale of its own town. Right: Skipton High Street. But from the shop signs you could be anywhere in England.

Not all the new building in Skipton is as sympathetic: ironically, the headquarters of the local building society is an out-of-scale monster. But the high street is still attractive, notwithstanding the forces of uniformity that are, inevitably, at work even here. Chain stores with their ugly shop-front designs *do* corrode local identity.

Craven Court is a new shopping centre. I rather like the way the developers have roofed over an old street and made it resemble an arcade. It's a bit like a covered market, which is very much a Yorkshire tradition.

It is encouraging to see a place like Skipton holding its own, so to speak, architecturally. But its people will have to be vigilant. The forces of change will continue to threaten Skipton – as they threaten all the great cities of Britain.

Below: The architect Jim Whale put a Victorian-looking roof over an old street to make Craven Court (left) an attractive place to go shopping. Critics will mutter 'pastiche' knowingly, but it's proving a great success.

Left: Symbol of civic pride: Leeds Town Hall, seen here in 1978, was designed by local architect Cuthbert Brodrick in the 1850s. It still holds its own on the skyline despite the encircling monuments to 'progress'.

Above: The vast, fortress-like Quarry Hill flats in Leeds (opened in 1938) were inspired by the heroic associations of the Karl Marx Hof: pioneer 'worker housing' in Vienna, where insurrectionists held out against the forces of a right-wing government in 1934. The Quarry Hill flats were demolished in 1978.

Leeds, not many miles away from Skipton, was a pioneer of comprehensive redevelopment in this country over fifty years ago and its historic character was consequently terribly damaged. But it kept its markets and arcades as a reminder of the Victorian past, and of the ways people used to do their shopping. Places like the Kirkgate market surely must have made the routine business of shopping a pleasure.

Developers always use an artist's impression to seduce us into the 'Brave New Shopping World'. But in reality, this New World turns out to be a kind of clinical laboratory where we are made to do our shopping. Even if we are a nation of shopkeepers, we can still, surely, be a nation of good architects!

Wherever I go I see the changes that are taking place, and engulfing our towns and cities. We have to remember that we *can* make choices about what is happening now. We *can* make something better of this second chance.

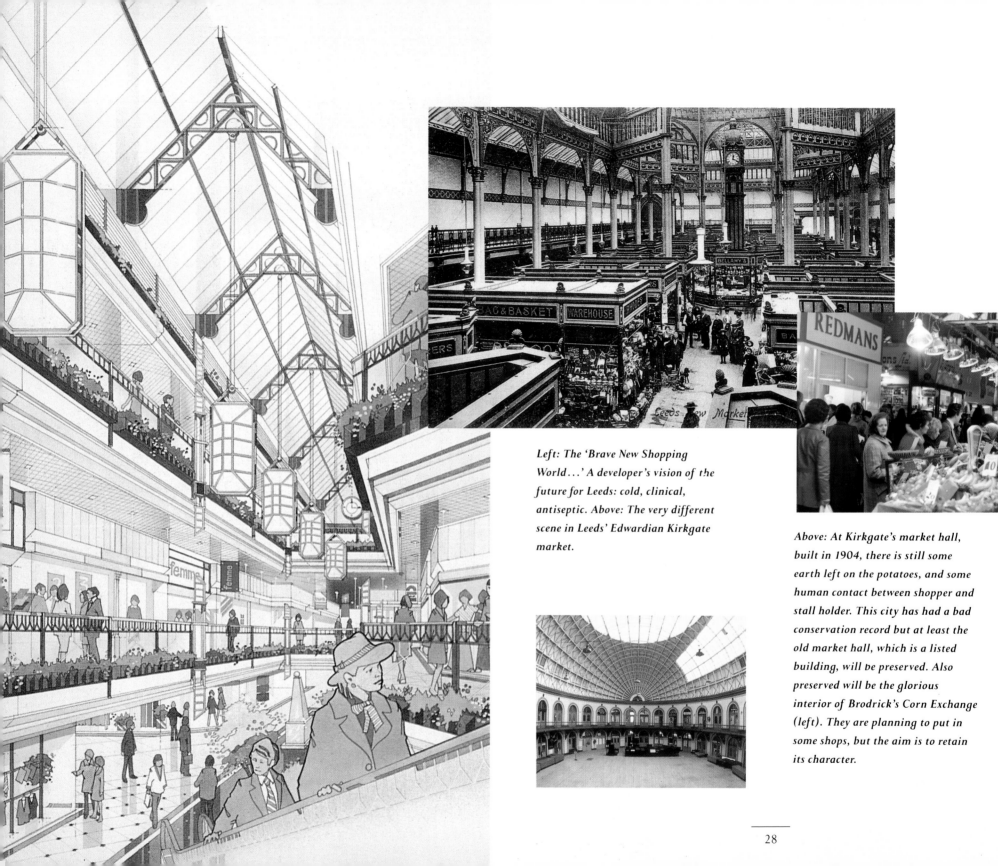

Left: The 'Brave New Shopping World . . .' A developer's vision of the future for Leeds: cold, clinical, antiseptic. Above: The very different scene in Leeds' Edwardian Kirkgate market.

Above: At Kirkgate's market hall, built in 1904, there is still some earth left on the potatoes, and some human contact between shopper and stall holder. This city has had a bad conservation record but at least the old market hall, which is a listed building, will be preserved. Also preserved will be the glorious interior of Brodrick's Corn Exchange (left). They are planning to put in some shops, but the aim is to retain its character.

*Right: The new Lion and Lamb
Yard in Farnham: shops (with offices
above them) that fit comfortably
into an old Surrey market town. The
unobtrusive shop signs and the
pleasantly enclosed sense of space
harmonise with, rather than destroy,
the fabric of the town. Below: What
we get too often in our towns: the
monumentally blank Friary
shopping centre in nearby Guildford.*

Above: Swansea Docks have already been transformed, and a maritime museum and arts centre, shops and housing, have brought life back to an area of decay and neglect.

Right: Edwardian Cardiff: rich in reminders of the city's prosperous past. The City Hall by Lanchester and Rickards (1897–1906).

Cardiff, the capital of Wales, gained its wealth from iron and the coal from the Welsh valleys which was exported round the world from Cardiff Bay. Here is a good example of what is happening to a city that still has an air of Edwardian prosperity in its architecture.

Cardiff is going to develop what they call a 'Marine City' in and around the docks, which are now derelict. With courage and vision something of real character could be built there. It would be a tragedy to allow in Cardiff what has happened in too many of our other ports, where fine historic warehouses and basins have been wantonly destroyed or filled in because of the speed of development or a lack of imagination. Cardiff's plans – only vague at the moment – give an indication that the new buildings will be inspired by the architecture of the city's past. I do hope they are.

There are huge plans afoot to build on a massive scale in and around Cardiff's old docklands. Above: An impression of the barrage they propose to build across Cardiff Bay, which will make possible a new 'Marine City' (below). There are some local fears about the effect the barrage will have on the ecology of the bay.

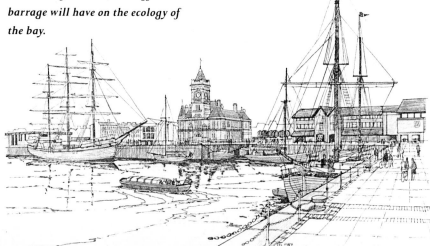

Birmingham is another story. It is a good lesson in how *not* to redevelop. All over Birmingham, which was once the manufacturing heart of the Empire, are derelict industrial sites. Now Birmingham wants to win back the old prosperity, and a huge swathe of new building is going up, slicing through the city, to attract new service industries. At the heart of it will be a vast convention centre, bigger than any other in Britain.

Above: Birmingham's Central Library. But how can you tell? It looks to me like a place where books are incinerated, not kept! Built in 1973 in Paradise Circus, it is an ill-mannered essay in concrete 'brutalism' intended to shock (which it certainly does). An insult to the grand civic buildings amongst which it squats.

Above: The new library took the place of the Victorian Mason College: an exuberant example of the Gothic Revival. Buildings like this testified to the confidence that Birmingham's citizens felt in their city, *and the importance they attached to public buildings during its most prosperous period. Left: The wasteland left by the collapse of Birmingham's traditional industries.*

Below: The site and (right) the model of the new International Convention Centre; there will be a huge hotel, sports halls, offices and shops. '…an unmitigated disaster' I remarked when I saw it, chiefly because the development turns its back so sadly on one of the last remnants of character in Birmingham, around the old canal.

I'm not against development, but I must confess I felt terribly demoralised when I went there to see the plans. Choosing my words to be as inoffensive as possible, I said I thought it was an unmitigated disaster. The development turns its back on Birmingham's Victorian past – it succeeds in making the buildings round the marvellous and under-appreciated canal seem like pathetic refugees. Birmingham's great public buildings look snubbed – doubly snubbed, because the city was wrecked once before in the 1950s and 60s. Because of such lack of vision, Birmingham's city centre became a monstrous concrete maze where only cars felt at home. People were bound to feel lost. Cars were placed above people and people were placed one above another on concrete shelves.

*Above: The heart of Birmingham:
the last rebuilding in the 60s led to
this: the triumph of the motor car,
with roads and car parks obliterating
every vestige of the old city.*

The Bull Ring, Birmingham

*Above: The Bull Ring in
the eighteenth century,
apparently a place of
almost bucolic calm.
Right: The Bull Ring in
1950 – alive with shoppers,
traffic and stall holders
shouting their wares;
typical of marketplaces all
over Britain as they once
were, and sometimes
(rarely) still are.*

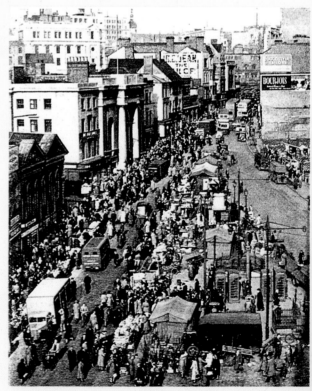

Left: The Bull Ring now...

Below: The most recent plan for the new Bull Ring, modified since my film (right). I hope that some of the old life can be put back into Birmingham.

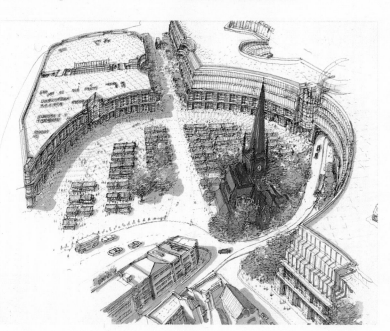

The Bull Ring today has no charm, no human scale, no character except arrogance. It's a planned accident. Most of it is coming down – thank goodness! So here is a second chance to put things right. But are we going to take it?

Anyone can build in a thoroughly unimaginative way. The secret, I believe, lies in creating surroundings which people are attracted to because they have that elusive something extra – what we call character. Apart from anything else, it makes commercial sense. The value of a development is enhanced if you create an attractive environment. Surely, after the experience of the last twenty years, we can get away from these terrible comprehensive development schemes?

The dream and the reality

Top: The problem:
Old Stepney. Mile after
mile of decaying slums
where disease, poverty and
blight corroded human
lives. Above: After the
remedy. After the slums
(and many thousands of
perfectly good houses as
well) have been cleared,
and mile after mile of new
housing estates have been
built, young residents
listlessly contemplate the
prospect before them.
Right: 'Bliss was it in that
dawn to be alive...' The
Mayor of Southwark hands
over the keys to thrilled new
tenants of the Brandon
Estate.

Above: Home Secretary Herbert
Morrison enjoys a joke with the Lord
Mayor of London and assorted
mayors while viewing the model of
the LCC Redevelopment Plan for
London in 1943.

Left: Soho development plan, 1950. The notorious modernist architect and planner Le Corbusier would have been impressed by this comprehensive scheme to demolish Soho and Oxford Street and rebuild on 'rationalist', 'scientific' and 'socially responsible' lines. Below: When part of Ronan Point collapsed in 1968, causing two deaths, it was the beginning of the end for the dream.

Many other blocks of flats, with a little assistance, were to follow Ronan Point. The Chelmsley Estate near Solihull (above three photographs) was blown up in 1989. There were few mourners.

It was of course not just commercial centres that suffered from out-of-scale, inhuman comprehensive development. The whole area of public housing was drastically affected by this architectural fashion. Bow, in London's Borough of Hackney, has one of the biggest housing estates of its kind in London. Only twenty years after its creation there are plans to replace this anonymous concrete wasteland with something better. A cynic might say that anything would be better, but it is a mammoth task.

One of the local Bow councillors explained the situation very clearly. He told me, 'Our problems are very different from those of Spitalfields. They have a difficulty with old Victorian slum dwellings and sweat shops. In Bow it is the things which replaced the Victorian slum dwellings – the 60s estates – which are our problem. Most of Bow consists of 1960s and early 70s estates which are producing horrendous problems. The best thing we can do is try and demolish as many of them as we can and replace them with brick-built houses with gardens which is obviously what the vast majority of tenants want.'

Left: Bow today: 'anything would be better...' The bitter legacy of comprehensive development. The victory of ideology and arrogance over humanity and common sense. Now the demolition men have moved in. Above: Bow tomorrow? An artist's impression of the new housing they want to build. It may not win any architectural awards, but I suspect people will like it. They don't, I find on the whole, want to live up in the sky, although provided the lifts and the management system work properly, elderly and single people sometimes seem to appreciate such an elevated existence.

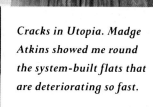

Cracks in Utopia. Madge Atkins showed me round the system-built flats that are deteriorating so fast.

Albany Place in Bow will represent a collaboration between a council and a private developer – and it looks like a good example of private and public sectors working together. This is certainly something I've been trying to encourage. Not all the blocks are coming down yet, but building work is ready to begin. Soon there will be streets here of small houses with their own gardens, just as there used to be.

In one of the flats Mrs Madge Atkins, the Albany Place Residents' Representative, told me about some of the problems with the old blocks. She showed me brackets which were holding the ceiling to the wall. 'The flat doesn't look too bad now but we've had a fight to do it... these brackets actually are holding the ceiling to the wall. The gap that was there was about an inch and a half before we had the brackets put in and the water just poured in. The window-frames were falling out... they've had about four window-frames that have fallen out straight onto the pavement... They have tried putting window-frames in but the concrete's no good so it doesn't hold the frames – so it's cheaper to pull them down and put new places up.'

Below: Lending a hand to the demolition process. I am told that crushed tower block, mixed with soil, makes a very good basis for growing roses.

Left: All over Britain local councils were subsidised to build gaunt and unlovely towers which rose like great tombstones from pointless and windswept open spaces, like these in Newcastle.

It's harder than it looks to knock down modern buildings. I was asked to help demolish an old car park on the estate and was glad to do so if it drew attention to Bow's attempts to do something better. I was amazed that a structure which looks as though it's falling apart at the seams should be so hard to knock down. To me, it was exactly like launching a ship or something when the bottle doesn't break. There was a wonderful 1920s film I saw with Mrs Eleanor Roosevelt trying to launch an aeroplane with a bottle. She hit it and nothing happened; a huge aide-de-camp came up to help but couldn't break it either – he just made a hole in the front of the aeroplane's nose...

As I hammered away at the car park, it occurred to me that this was a symbol of the whole

sad legacy of 60s housing – an up-to-date dinosaur that was born extinct. A colossal fossil. It was never alive, but it hangs on like grim death.

The Houses of Parliament (seen left in a late-19th-century painting by George V. Cole) were inspired by a vision of order and beauty. The classical plan is dressed in the robes of Gothic history and enriched with the finest craftsmanship.

To see the devastating effect that so much of the new architecture has had on London I took a trip down the Thames with Christopher Booker. He was one of the first writers to visit some of the prizewinning high-rise housing to find out if the lifts were working. Usually they weren't.

The Houses of Parliament look particularly wonderful since they've been cleaned – you see the full glory of them now. As Christopher Booker pointed out, 'It is a building unlike any other in the world. In a way you can say it's an office block – and yet, architecturally, it's a thing of extraordinary beauty and power.'

The banks of the Thames have long been the setting for palaces both royal and civic. The tradition continued from Somerset House in the eighteenth century (top), by Sir William Chambers, to County Hall (above) designed by Ralph Knott at the beginning of this century. The Festival of Britain in 1951 put palaces of culture on the Thames. The National Theatre – perhaps more like a bunker than a palace – followed the fashion for concrete in the 70s (facing page). Architect Terry Farrell has ambitious schemes (below and left) to cheer up the concrete gulag of an arts complex that the festival site became, and American architects SOM are transforming County Hall (right) into an hotel, flats and offices.

The river today is a far cry from the glorious scene depicted by Constable (above) when Waterloo Bridge opened in 1817.

Wordsworth saw a view from Westminster Bridge that inspired him to write:

Earth has not anything to show more fair:
Dull would he be of soul who could pass by
A sight so touching in its majesty:
This City now doth, like a garment, wear
The beauty of the morning; silent, bare,
Ships, towers, domes, theatres, and temples lie
Open unto the fields, and to the sky;
All bright and glittering in the smokeless air.   (1802)

Just beyond Westminster Bridge lies one of *our* contributions to that view. The National Theatre seems like a clever way of building a nuclear power station in the middle of London without anyone objecting. I try very hard, I must say, to persuade myself to appreciate this sort of architecture, but I can't.

Above: Generously London's post-war planners allow us this glimpse of St Paul's from the river. Below: How amazing to think this excrescence, Mondial House, passed through any kind of planning process. Do humans work in there?

A bit further down the river the post-war planners allow us just a glimpse of St Paul's Cathedral. The lack of sensitivity about the immediate surroundings of St Paul's is extraordinary. I can't understand why people didn't feel that in such an important area it would be right to complement St Paul's with buildings that harmonise with, rather than scream at, the main building itself. I find it incomprehensible that such a vital matter wasn't given proper consideration.

As you continue down the river, it is poignant that you can only just glimpse Wren's Monument to the Great Fire as you pass the dreadful Mondial House. To me this building is redolent of a word processor. I don't see that people particularly want a perpetual view of a word processor when they find themselves living with them all the time in the office or at home.

The ruination of Wren's London started before the Luftwaffe arrived. It began in the 1920s when the cliff face of Adelaide House (left), a strange Egyptian-style hulk of offices, dwarfed the spire of Wren's St Magnus Martyr. The Roman Doric column of the Monument to the Great Fire of London just retains its dignity, but not its dominance, alongside the angular awkwardness of the National Westminster Bank Tower.

Almost opposite the Tower of London is the site for the second phase of London Bridge City, where three competing schemes revealed the current architectural dilemma: what do you build by the Thames? Venetian (top) by John Simpson? Anonymous modern (centre) by Twigg Brown? Or romantic (but rather superficial) Gothic Revival (bottom) by Philip Johnson and John Burgee?

Above: The poor old Tower of London itself lies somewhere here, remorselessly buried by the crude mass of the Tower Hotel and overshadowed by the slovenly towers of commerce.

I try very hard to appreciate the sort of skyline that has been imposed on the City, but I can't. There's no doubt in my mind that something like a spire or a dome, something which gives an inspired finish to the top of a building, has the effect of raising one's spirits in a remarkable way. Presumably Wordsworth was affected in the same sort of way when he composed his poem 'Upon Westminster Bridge'. I can't believe that he would feel the same about the City skyline today.

Artists in the nineteenth century saw beauty in the London riverside: not just in the traditional views of St Paul's Cathedral (far right: mid-19th-century view of the city by John Gendall), but also in the booming Docklands (above: Tower Bridge in 1898 by C.E. Dixon). The view (right) that artist William Daniell recorded in 1803 of the great port of the Empire has now vanished forever.

London's Docklands are undergoing substantial changes. There are only small areas left that show London's river as it was, with the kind of buildings along the banks of the Thames which allowed views of the City beyond. The roof heights were on a more human scale and behind them you had visions of the churches and spires rising above the chimneys and the roofs.

Once the warehouses of a great trading empire stood along the banks, and on the river ships from all over the world docked. Dare I say it, mightn't we have used them as an inspiration and risen to the challenge?

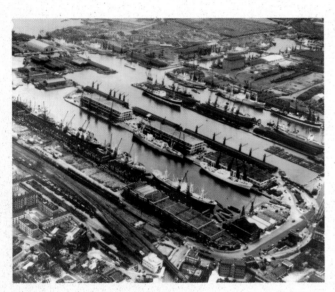

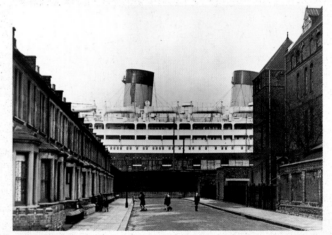

London's Docklands before their recent transformation were scaled to the size of the ships that used them. Canary Wharf (above), wool cargoes (top right) and ships such as the Dominion Monarch in the King George V Dock (right) were all visible witness in the capital to Britain's mastery of the seas.

The new Docklands of the 1980s show the triumph of commercial expediency over civic values. Too many mediocre buildings, and a railway suitable only for Toytown (bottom right) represent a feeble contribution to the rebuilding of the capital. A wasted opportunity where indifferent commerce snubs the deprived boroughs all around Docklands. Right: The aggressive-looking Cascades housing development seems to me inappropriately high. I personally think the edge of the river should be more sacrosanct.

Docklands is an 'Enterprise Zone', however. To get business moving, the normal planning regulations aren't applied here. Consequently there has been a lot of rather hurried development. Within the area is what promises to be the largest commercial development in Europe – Canary Wharf. I had an opportunity to view the models in London. The eased planning regulations mean that the developers are able to build what could be the tallest tower block in Europe – 800 feet high. The same developers are responsible for massive schemes in Toronto and New York.

Top: The monstrous Canary Wharf –
one of the highest towers in Europe
– is a monument to the wrong
thinking of the 1960s, but built

in the 1980s. Battery Park City in
New York (above) is by the same
architect: spot the difference...

I had a discussion with Cesar Pelli, the architect of the tower. I asked him if it was the first time he'd done a project in this country. He replied, 'Yes, it's the very first time, so it took a great deal of thinking about how one should approach the problem here in England. It needs to be done with assurance. I feel that occupying this place against the sky is a bit like being on stage and one cannot be fumbling on stage, one has to be self-assured.'

I asked him why it had to be quite so high. He told me, 'There are two issues. One is that a certain size is required by modern institutions. They need to have a certain number of people close to each other, which is interesting. As technology develops people seem to be needing to be near each other physically more and more. But there is also clearly a certain desire just to be high, so that the building has a certain prominence against the sky.'

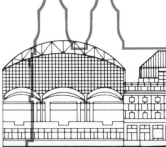

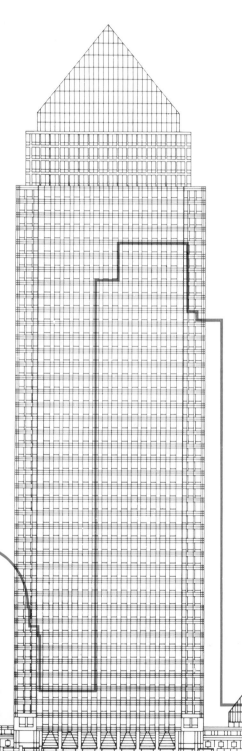

This drawing shows the size of this out-of-scale obelisk in relation to St Paul's and the NatWest Tower – the tallest building in England. It is wrong for London and will wreck the famous view north from Greenwich painted by Turner in 1809 (below). He called the spires he saw from Greenwich 'gleams of hope amidst a world of care'. What hope for London now? Cesar Pelli's tower may become the tomb of modernistic dogma. The tragedy is that it will cast its shadow over generations of Londoners who have suffered enough from towers of architectural arrogance.

But I think that, in this country, things have always been on a more intimate scale. In the United States you almost expect a tower block like Cesar Pelli's to rise up out of the plains of Texas. I personally would go mad if I had to work in a building like that. It is the size and density of Canary Wharf that has caused such a stir, and the impact it will have on the London skyline – in particular the famous view north from Greenwich – that is the problem.

This is a view that Turner painted, looking beyond the twin towers of Christopher Wren's Greenwich Hospital towards the City. It is not easy nowadays to remember how Wren's City churches used to surround the glorious dome of St Paul's, like so many yachts riding at anchor around a great ship. It was a skyline inviolate when Canaletto painted it *(overleaf)*, and the vista was still substantially intact right up to 1960.

London used to be one of the architectural wonders of the world, a city built on the water like the centre of another great trading empire, Venice. And when Canaletto painted it in the 18th century, it was no less beautiful.

The London that slowly evolved after the Great Fire took more than three hundred years to build. It took about fifteen years to destroy. What was rebuilt after the war has succeeded in wrecking London's skyline and spoiling the view of St Paul's in a jostling scrum of skyscrapers, all competing for attention.

Above: German bombers over London, 1940. Below: The damage caused by the Blitz revived memories of the Great Fire of London of 1666 (right) and cleared the way, some people felt, for a major rebuilding.

Above: In 1930 St Paul's dome still sailed above the City.

Above: In 1960 the rising rot had started with a vengeance.

Above: By 1989 the soul of the City has been conquered by the hovering hordes of concrete giants. Right: Compare Paris where Notre Dame serenely points against a clear sky to an uncluttered Heaven.

Can you imagine the French doing this sort of thing in Paris, on the banks of the Seine around Notre Dame? Or the Venetians building tower blocks next to San Marco? When did we lose our sense of vision? How could those in control become so out of step with so many Londoners who felt powerless to resist the destruction of their City? There is no need for London to ape Manhattan. We already possessed a skyline. They had to create one. And there is no need for buildings, just because they house computers and word processors, to look like machines themselves.

In newer countries than ours there was perhaps more point in architects creating dramatic skylines, and such cities as these, where skyscrapers and adventurous forms do not smother and dwarf the past in quite the same way as they do in Britain, undoubtedly have a powerful presence. How humane they are to work and live in is another question. Sydney (top), Dallas (above), Pittsburgh (right).

Right and below right: In Vancouver the buildings are not quite like those of Dallas or Houston in Texas, but they echo the same great North American dream in the language of their architecture and the absence of any clear local tradition on which to draw. San Gimignano in Tuscany is often quoted as the forerunner of Manhattan – 'if it was done by the Renaissance Italians then it must be all right' – but as far as I'm concerned, any similarities are coincidental!

Property developers in the 80s
realised the value of large acreages
of railway lands, particularly in
London. Behind King's Cross
terminal (right and far right) more
than 100 acres are to become one of
the largest property developments in
Europe. There are signs (below) that
architect Norman Foster may produce
a brilliantly engineered new
terminal for Channel Tunnel trains.
Will the rest of the development
match the quality of our great
railway heritage? The opportunities
at King's Cross are phenomenal.
Improving conditions for the
surrounding community should be a
priority, and careful consultations
are essential to avoid just another

rehash of so many of London's recent
developments. Air-rights building,
that is to say building over roads and
railways where there is still some
space left, is a new phenomenon in
London. At Cannon Street (top,
facing page) they are filling in the
space above the station.

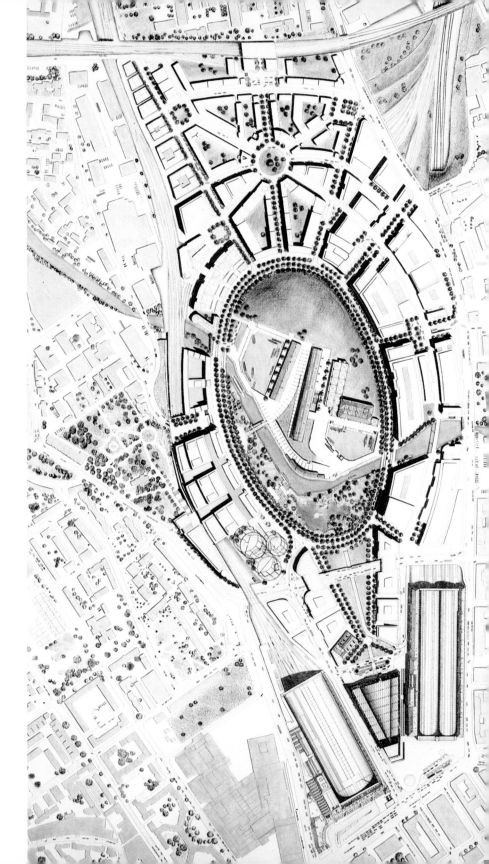

Right: At Charing Cross art deco lives again over the railway station. Left: At London Wall offices sprout over existing roads. Both schemes are designed by Terry Farrell in a transatlantic post-modern style.

One of the City's main functions is to create wealth, but surely there should also be an obligation to spend some of that money on buildings that are beautiful, that are a pleasure to look at – and to work in. We should have architecture that celebrates London's mercantile success, and then *humanises* it.

There is probably far more development going on in London now than there was in the 60s. It is nothing less than a great rebuilding over large parts of the capital. I wonder how much say the general public is having in it? How good is all this new development?

Right: Robert Smirke's glorious domed Reading Room in the British Museum links learning to its classical roots. 'What peace, what love, what truth, what beauty...' wrote Thackeray, 'are here spread out.' Below: The Reading Room in the new British Library by Professor Colin St John Wilson is without resonance. 'Love', 'truth' and 'beauty' have fled.

What happened to pride in our national institutions? Above: The multi-million-pound British Library is a dim collection of brick sheds groping for some symbolic significance. People will think that the Gothic St Pancras is the library and this is the new railway station.

The BBC should be a public patron of the best architects. Left: The first stage of the new headquarters at White City. I suppose that commercial expediency has led the Corporation to opt for a cheaper, utilitarian solution, and to settle for mediocrity. I hope their nerve will return for stage two.

Take the new British Library. How can you even tell that it *is* a library? It has no character to suggest that it is a great public building. And the Reading Room looks more like the assembly hall of an academy for secret police. It could not contrast more sharply with what it's replacing – the beautiful old Reading Room in the British Museum which even Karl Marx had to admit did some credit to the capitalist society he sat there plotting to overthrow.

Having made a film for the BBC, I'd like to be a bit more enthusiastic about what they are building at White City. The BBC is a great cultural institution. I would have hoped that their sense of responsibility would have extended beyond their programmes and been more evident in this, their most recent addition to the capital. It may not be in the centre of town, but it still matters just as much.

A subject of two monumental public enquiries is the Mappin & Webb site in a conservation area at the heart of the City. There are plans to pull it down and replace it with a building which, I think, looks rather like an old 1930s wireless. But why pull down one of the few remaining bits of the Victorian City, including no fewer than eight listed buildings, at all? What on earth is the point of having conservation areas if we are going to disregard them?

Left: J. and J. Belcher's Mappin & Webb building, with its Franco-Flemish curved tower, is one of the City's best surviving examples of Victorian commercial architecture.

Once it was to be demolished for a Mies van der Rohe 'glass stump' and now it looks as if it's going to be replaced with James Stirling's monumental edifice (above).

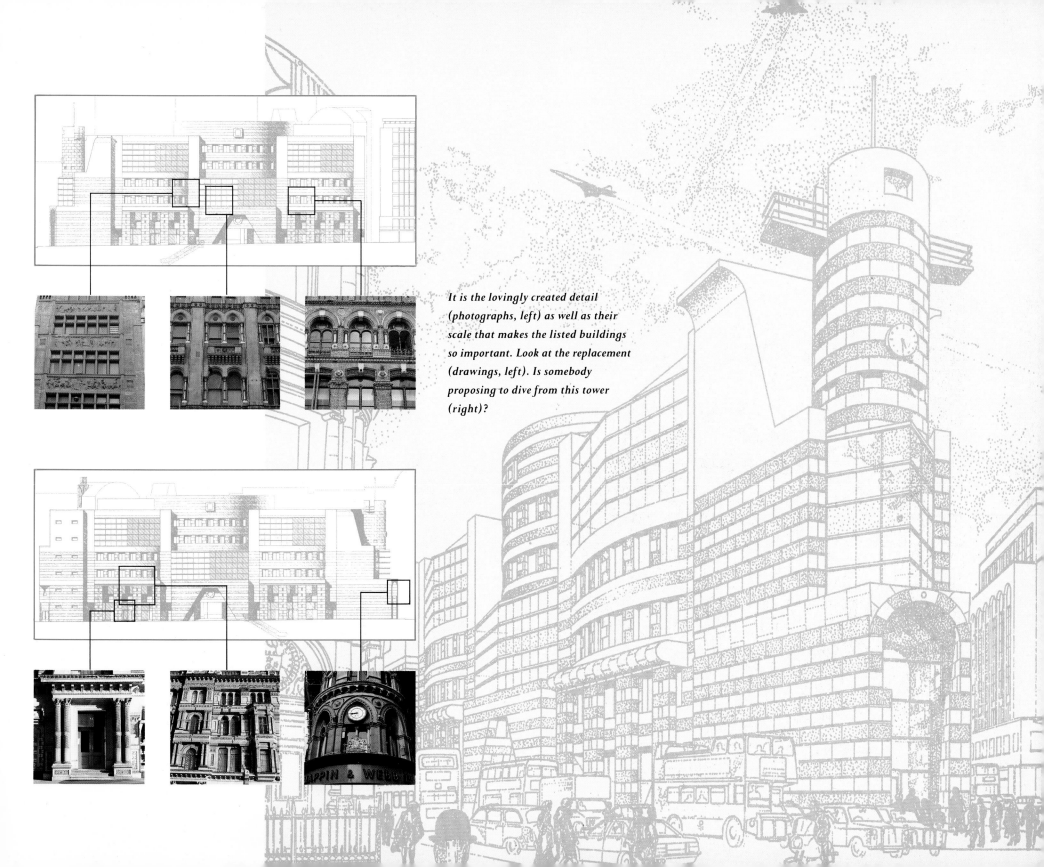

It is the lovingly created detail (photographs, left) as well as their scale that makes the listed buildings so important. Look at the replacement (drawings, left). Is somebody proposing to dive from this tower (right)?

Left and model below: Paternoster Square as we see it today is the post-war dream of architect and planner Lord Holford and a City Corporation that wanted a New City after the war. It is architecturally indifferent and out of scale with Wren's cathedral.

And then, next to St Paul's Cathedral, there's Paternoster Square. Paternoster Square was the prototype for all the windswept urban squares dreamt up in the 50s and 60s. Now it looks as if it may come down too.

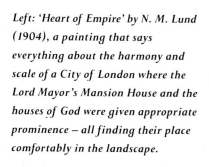

Left: 'Heart of Empire' by N. M. Lund (1904), a painting that says everything about the harmony and scale of a City of London where the Lord Mayor's Mansion House and the houses of God were given appropriate prominence – all finding their place comfortably in the landscape.

Paternoster proposals

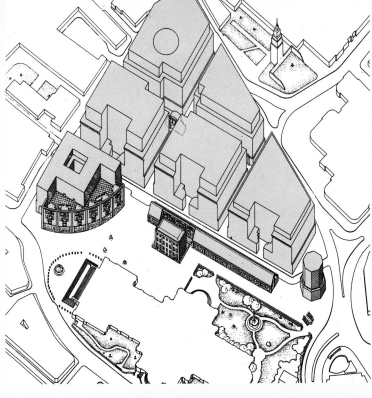

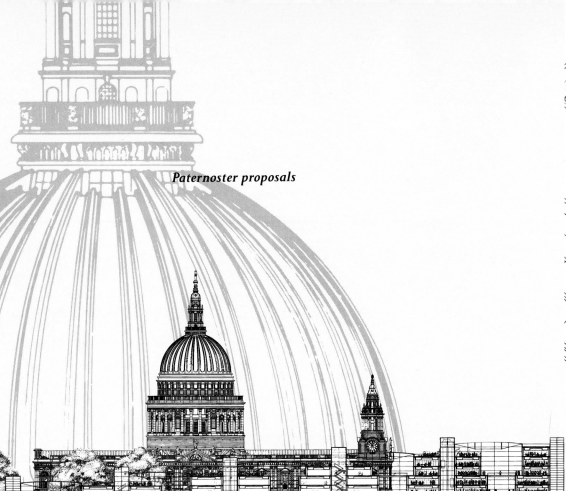

The 1987 developers'
competition produced
designs by some of the
world's leading architects.
The entries of Norman
Foster (above and left),
James Stirling (top right),
and Arata Isozaki (above
right and right), all failed
to do justice to the cathedral,
and demonstrated how wrong
the original brief was.

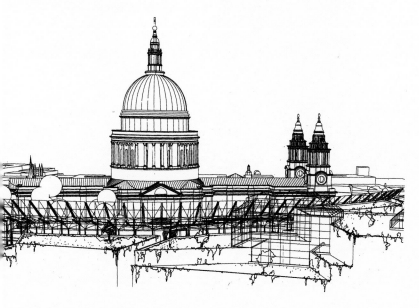

Above: Arup Associates, who won the developers' competition, seemed to want to put St Paul's in a prison camp, surrounding it with this spiky roof-line.

When I saw the developer's initial concept for a replacement, I must confess that I was deeply depressed. It didn't seem to rise to the occasion. This site is next to our great national cathedral – the very heart of the capital city. What place in Britain could be more important? Paternoster Square was something that I felt I had to speak up about.

I did so in a speech at London's Mansion House on 1st December 1987: 'Surely here, if anywhere, was the time and place to sacrifice some profit, if need be, for generosity of vision, for elegance, for dignity; for buildings which would raise our spirits and our faith in commercial enterprise, and prove that capitalism can have a human face.'

Above and right: The model of Arup's revised design: an exercise in watered-down classicism. The curved façade has superficial attraction as an idea, but on closer inspection it becomes less attractive. It is a rather half-hearted, grudging attempt to accommodate public concern about the national importance of this great site.

As I anticipated, there was rather an interesting row after I said all that. But it instantly became clear that I wasn't speaking just for myself. Since the speech, there have been two exhibitions in the crypt of St Paul's. The outline scheme by Arup Associates held centre stage. The public at least managed a look-in for once. At the first exhibition there was another plan on display – by John Simpson, an architect who works within the classical tradition. His starting point was the original street pattern and his buildings defer to St Paul's. The public certainly seemed to prefer the traditional materials and the far more human scale of Simpson's scheme.

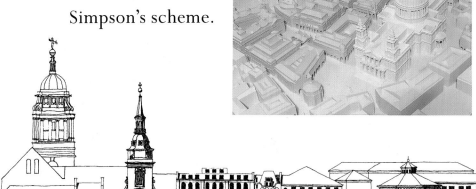

John Simpson is not afraid to design in a serious and appropriate classical style to defer to the cathedral. Like Wren he sees the surroundings of St Paul's as a humane, brick and stone collection of carefully detailed buildings. Above: Carl Laubin's painting shows how such buildings might look, as does the model (left) and the drawing (below) which also give an idea of the sheer size of the project.

This kind of design is all too often ridiculed as 'pastiche'. People use the word disparagingly. They mean 'fake' or a direct copy, something utterly unimaginative. But there's nothing 'fake' about building in an established tradition, or in trying to revive one. And there's nothing anti-technological about classical architecture either.

People say you can't house up-to-date office space, with all its ducts and cables, behind a neo-Georgian or more traditional façade. Well, I've looked into this, and you *can*. Paternoster Square has become central to the argument between modernist and traditional architecture, or, as I'd rather put it, the argument between the inhuman and the human.

The City needs a coherent plan for the area around St Paul's, but it must be one that puts people first and re-creates the scale and atmosphere so well captured in this nineteenth-century painting by John O'Connor.

A VISION OF BRITAIN

TEN PRINCIPLES

HRH THE PRINCE OF WALES

TEN PRINCIPLES

WE CAN BUILD UPON

While I was carrying out the research for my film on architecture, I became increasingly aware of the failure of the current planning rules and regulations to create a better environment. It is not that there is any shortage of red tape: after all, every building that has been put up since 1947 has had planning permission, except for those associated with agriculture and Government activities. It's hard to believe sometimes, but the whole contemporary, built world has been through the mill of bureaucracy, committees, negotiations, often long and expensive public enquiries. To what end, I often ask myself? I can only say that from the thousands of letters I receive it is clear that vast numbers of people are equally puzzled.

It seemed to me that it might be worth looking into this question, so I canvassed the views and advice of all sorts of people with a profound interest in the subject, and the result has been distilled into a new set of suggested ground rules. By standing back and looking at what has been happening as objectively as possible, I could see that we seem to have forgotten some of the basic principles that have governed architecture since the Greeks. Many of them are simple common sense, like the laws of grammar that create a language.

I would suggest that if you destroy the past, or consistently deny its relevance to the present, man eventually loses his soul and his roots. In order to avoid repeating the obvious mistakes of the last forty or fifty years it is essential to appreciate that certain values and principles are eternal ones, in terms of human experience. Because our technology changes so rapidly it does not mean our spirits, or our fundamental psychological responses, alter as well. Being modern and up-to-date does not mean we have to invent a new style or some new, revolutionary building material every other year.

We do not have to live in surroundings which directly reflect the latest sophisticated technology. Apart from anything else, such forms of design tend to ignore natural conditions (climatic and otherwise) and are frequently energy-inefficient. (Think of huge office blocks with their vast expanses of glass, and the energy required to heat and air-condition them – not to mention the effect on the ozone layer from the CFCs contained in the air-conditioning systems!)

Above all, it seems to me that we have suffered too long from the imposition of a kind of nondescript, mediocre, synthetic, international style of architecture which is found everywhere – from Riyadh to Rangoon. Our own heritage of regional styles and individual characteristics has been eaten away by this creeping cancer, and I would suggest the time is ripe to rediscover the extraordinary richness of our architectural past, as well as the basic principles which allowed our much-loved towns and villages to develop as they did.

If we follow this course we can still remain modern, up-to-date and contemporary in terms of our technological approach to life, while at the same time satisfying intangible needs of the spirit. These needs have unconsciously been responsible for everything of any beauty in our man-made surroundings since human beings first abandoned their caves and began to construct dwellings.

Why, I ask you, do so many people flock to those countries where beautiful towns and villages and landscapes still exist? Why do so many architects, planners and developers frequent such places on their holidays? Why do sightseers and tourists in this country visit what is left of our old towns and villages rather than rush off to see the centre of Birmingham or Cumbernauld? Why, for example, is the Architectural Association's headquarters situated in one of London's most beautiful 18th-century squares, while some of its graduates have been helping to create ever uglier surroundings for other people to live in? The answer is because our forebears, to the last man, understood and followed an accepted set of ground rules.

Although I'll be criticised for my ideas I'm sure there is a general agreement that an emphasis on quality creates greater value, as well as leaving our descendants something worth inheriting. What follows, therefore, is not new. It is a simple extension of the rules and patterns that have guided architects and builders for centuries. I hope it may be a timely reminder.

Today almost all new buildings are provided by private companies. It is a sad fact that very few of the patrons of new buildings, whether they be private or public, have any aesthetic ambitions. Most of them are quite unaware of their awesome responsibilities and their remarkable opportunities.

It isn't up to me to rewrite the planning laws, but I do think it might help if we sat back for a moment and looked at the whole process. It seems to me that we are lost in a maze of regulations; perhaps the way out is simpler than we think. I'm sure that the man in the street knows exactly what he wants, but he is frustrated by form-filling and the mystique that surrounds the professionals. I want to see laymen and professionals working together; developers, architects and craftsmen understanding each other. I want to demolish the barriers of bureaucracy, and discover that common ground we seem to have lost. There is nothing wrong with simplicity.

Above: A church spire punctuates the flatness of the Fens, without disturbing their beauty.

Below: Large buildings should be broken down into smaller elements, rather than built as one out-of-scale lump.

Trentishoe, Devonshire

We must respect the land. It is our birthright and almost every inch of it is densely layered with our island history.

The landscape is the setting for all our architecture. In the United Kingdom we are blessed with an enormous variety of landscape. Such richness – from the hills of Derbyshire and the Yorkshire Dales to the level fens of Lincolnshire – is greatly to be treasured. Often the type of land is gentle and subtle and correspondingly delicate and easily damaged. Much has been damaged – the last war didn't help in this respect – but it can be restored if people are prepared to take the time and trouble.

New buildings can be intrusive or they can be designed and sited so that they fit in. It is seldom enough to disguise them by planting: the scale and nature of the new buildings are crucial. Rather than planning from a drawing board or plotting road routes on a map, we should feel the lie of the land and its contours and respect them as a result.

Above: The Metro Centre near Newcastle. The bulk of this building is divided up, but the concentration of shopping attracts a sea of cars. Right: No overhead wires in Burford, Oxfordshire. Below: Cartoon by Osbert Lancaster.

'Don't rape the landscape.'

New buildings should not dominate the landscape but blend carefully with it. Often large buildings can be separated into elements which will humanise the scale, give a gentler skyline and enhance the picturesque quality of our landscape.

We must protect the land. We need, for all sorts of complex historical and psychological reasons, to keep a sense of wilderness. The green belts are a valuable contribution to the preservation (even if sometimes this is an illusion) of the countryside. If new buildings avoid sprawl and are grouped together, more of the landscape can be preserved. There's no point, as I see it, in having green belts unless they are genuinely green. It would help, in a small island, to avoid the wirescape, the spread of sodium lighting, the rash of badly designed supermarkets and petrol stations and the fields full of parked cars. Farms and many Government buildings and structures such as army camps and power stations may be immune from planning laws, but they should not be immune from aesthetic considerations – they, above all, should respect the land.

Town Hall, Abingdon, Oxfordshire

There are two kinds of hierarchy which need concern us here. One is the size of buildings in relation to their public importance. The other is the relative significance of the different elements which make up a building – so that we know, for instance, where the front door is!

Buildings should reflect these hierarchies, for architecture is like a language. You cannot construct pleasing sentences in English unless you have a thorough knowledge of the grammatical ground rules. If you abandon these basic principles of grammar the result is discordant and inharmonious. Good architecture should be like good manners and follow a recognised code. Civilised life is made more pleasurable by a shared understanding of simple rules of conduct.

Above: Where is the civic pride, and where is the entrance, to Chippenham's council offices? Right: A public house in Islington draws attention to itself by its enrichment and slightly increased scale. Below right: The regular front of an Edwardian commercial building is modulated to show where the door is.

St Pancras, London

**'If a building can't express itself,
how can we understand it?'**

A good building that understands the rules explains itself in its forms and spaces, tells us where to go and what to expect. It emphasises those parts that are public and important. Even in the smallest house there is a distinction between back and front doors, between living-room and attic windows. Only in recent large buildings have we lost this sense of hierarchy, so that it is hard to discover whether the block at the end of the street is a hotel, office or civic centre.

Public buildings ought to proclaim themselves with pride, as they have in the past. A Doric portico on a bank, an elaborate window-trimming on the meeting room of the town hall, a generous and lofty entrance hall in an hotel all serve to set the scene and uplift our spirits. Nowadays the dogma of modernism ensures a deadening uniformity.

Public façades are not the only issue: there is also the need for some buildings to be bigger than others. There is a recognisable hierarchy in towns and villages that may seem obvious. Churches, public buildings, halls and pubs all have their scale and special sites. In a way they emphasise our values as well as our social organisations.

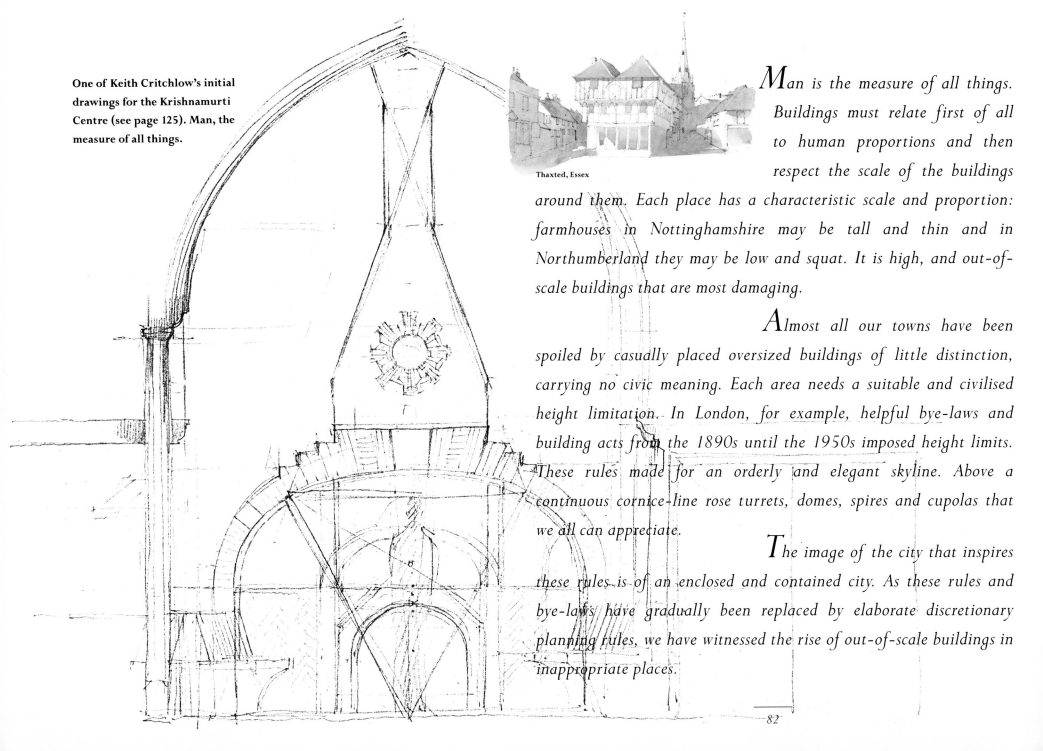

One of Keith Critchlow's initial drawings for the Krishnamurti Centre (see page 125). Man, the measure of all things.

Thaxted, Essex

*M*an is the measure of all things. Buildings must relate first of all to human proportions and then respect the scale of the buildings around them. Each place has a characteristic scale and proportion: farmhouses in Nottinghamshire may be tall and thin and in Northumberland they may be low and squat. It is high, and out-of-scale buildings that are most damaging.

*A*lmost all our towns have been spoiled by casually placed oversized buildings of little distinction, carrying no civic meaning. Each area needs a suitable and civilised height limitation. In London, for example, helpful bye-laws and building acts from the 1890s until the 1950s imposed height limits. These rules made for an orderly and elegant skyline. Above a continuous cornice-line rose turrets, domes, spires and cupolas that we all can appreciate.

*T*he image of the city that inspires these rules is of an enclosed and contained city. As these rules and bye-laws have gradually been replaced by elaborate discretionary planning rules, we have witnessed the rise of out-of-scale buildings in inappropriate places.

'Less might be more; too much is not enough.'

The redevelopment of towns and cities once respected plot sizes, existing street patterns, parks and squares. Today, far too often, developers are allowed to assemble several small sites, regurgitating them as gargantuan out-of-scale developments that look like Gulliver in Lilliput.

Sometimes a great public building may dominate a city, but it will be the sort of building that reflects our aspirations, like our great cathedrals. We raise to heaven that which is valuable to us: emblems of faith, enlightenment or government. But this vision must also be supported by small-scale buildings which reflect our intimate lives.

Top: This is sacrilege. Casually placed out-of-scale buildings dwarf Gloucester Cathedral. Above: Salisbury Cathedral has been shown due respect.

Bradford Town Hall

Marlborough, Wiltshire

Harmony is the playing together of the parts. Each building that goes beside another has to be in tune with its neighbour. A straggling village street or a wide city avenue which may consist of buildings belonging to many different periods can look harmonious.

Nowadays there seems to be too much insensitive infilling of a particularly jarring nature in our towns and villages. Buildings boast too much and forget their neighbours. We have lost that desire to fit in which was once so natural to us, and gave us some of our loveliest streets and compatible groups of buildings. Whatever happened to architects' and designers' humility?

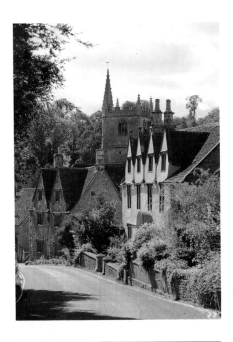

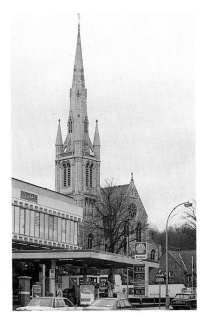

Above left: Concord in Castle Combe. Above right: Discord in Roehampton. Left: G.E. Street's late 19th-century law courts in London demonstrate how vast bulk can be scaled down and fitted into a city street.

Right: The Circus, Bath. The harmony of Bath is in the layout of its streets and squares as much as in the details of its buildings.

Top: The regular rhythm of Bedford Square in London is enlivened by its supporting elements, which also add to the sense of unity.

'Sing with the choir and not against it.'

Because of the scale of our country it is more necessary to respect our indigenous roots than to imitate transient international architectural fashions. Our older towns cannot easily absorb the more extreme examples of outlandish modern design. Perhaps we should give the best contemporary designs a sporting chance in our new towns?

Towns such as Cheltenham and Bath exemplify the virtues of architectural harmony, not only in their layout but in their organisation of the smaller architectural elements such as door cases, balconies, cornices and railings. It was second nature to the 18th-century architect to add one house to another with a sense of concord and unity.

Today buildings are designed from abstract principles and are thrust, in the name of 'new' architecture and 'modern' functional requirements, into the carefully scaled and painstakingly adjusted cities of the past. Their impact can be softened by an acceptance of the existing street rhythms and plot sizes. Buildings in a city such as Edinburgh are the individual brush strokes of a grand composition, because all the participants understand the basic rules and traditions. Harmony is the pleasing result.

ENCLOSURE

Almshouses, Froxfield, Wiltshire

One of the great pleasures of architecture is the feeling of well-designed enclosure. It is an elementary idea with a thousand variants and can be appreciated at every level of building from the individual room to the interior of St Paul's Cathedral, or from the grand paved public square to the walled garden.

The scale can be large or small, the materials ancient or modern, but cohesion, continuity and enclosure produce a kind of magic. The application of these ideas makes a place unique.

Above: Richmond in North Yorkshire: the English equivalent of the Sienese Campo. Right: A sense of enclosure in a short London street, Gordon Place. Far right: Collegiate tradition ensured that Nuffield College, Oxford, preserved a sense of enclosure into the 1950s.

Above: Lower Earley, Berkshire:
piled up for profit rather than
pleasure? There are few signs of a
chimney, by the way, or a window
of a different shape.

**'Give us somewhere safe for the
children to play and let the wind
play somewhere else.'**

*T*he secret of enclosed spaces is
that they should have few entrances; if there are too many the sense
of security disappears. If the space contains something to love such as
a garden, a sculpture or a fountain, it is more likely to be cherished
and not vandalised. A community spirit is born far more easily in a
well-formed square or courtyard than in a random scattering of
developers' plots. The squares, almshouses, universities and inns of
court of our past that we love so well have always answered our needs.
Their virtues are timeless, still providing privacy, beauty and a feeling
of total safety.

*S*urely we can apply some of these
lessons to the vast and neglected soulless deserts of post-war housing?
Our new housing estates need not always be strewn clusters of
separate houses set at jagged angles along windswept planners'
routes. Examples exist all around us of the ideal homes that people
have loved for ages: it is simply a matter of learning to imitate the
best. Discriminating observation of the past must be the inspiration
for the future. It is surely a worthwhile investment in many cases
to resurrect this age-old principle of enclosure which creates a
recognisable community of neighbours.

MATERIALS

Top left: Cob and thatch in Dorset.
Middle left: Clapboarding and tiles
in Kent. Bottom left: Pebbles by
the sea in Devon.

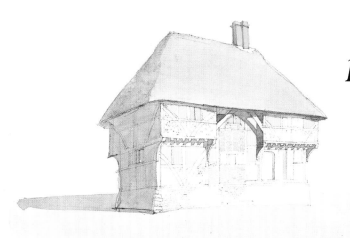

Wealden House, Sussex

Britain is one of the most geologically complicated countries in the world, and as a result it is one of the most beautiful. Our rich variety of building materials is a source of constant pleasure and surprise, for our villages and towns were built from what came closest to hand: stone in Northamptonshire, timber in Herefordshire, cob in Devon, flint in the Sussex downs, brick in Nottinghamshire. Each town and each village has a different hue, a different feel, and fosters a fierce loyalty in those who belong there. We must retain this feeling; we must ensure that local character is not permanently eroded.

While the 19th century saw the beginning of that erosion, the late 20th has brought a bland and standardised uniformity to our building materials. We can no longer tell where we are. Concrete, plastic cladding, aluminium, machine-made bricks and reconstituted stone are shipped to every corner of Britain from centralised production lines. This has created an overall mediocrity: a kind of architectural soap opera.

Top: Anonymous plastic cladding
which could be anywhere. Above:
The glitzy Odeon Cinema in
Sheffield has apparently descended
from outer space into the stone
Victorian centre.

*To enable new buildings to look as
though they belong, and thereby enhance the natural surroundings,
each district should have a detailed inventory of its local building
materials and the way in which they are used. This should become a
bible for local planning authorities and should be held up as a model
to developers and their architects.*

*Britain has to revive and nurture
its rural and individual urban characteristics based upon local
materials. Perhaps there is even a case for reopening some of our great
stone quarries. We must also encourage our traditional craftsmen
– our flint-knappers, our thatchers, our blacksmiths – and involve
them in the building of our future. This will in time engender an
economic revival which is not dependent on centralised industries but
which is locally based.*

Left: Workers at the Cat Castle
stone quarry, County Durham, in
1910. The quarry was closed down
in 1914, but reopened in 1977.

Kilpeck Church, Herefordshire

There seems to be a growing feeling that modern functional buildings with no hint of decoration give neither pleasure nor delight. The training of the modern architect rarely encompasses the rules of ornament or the study of past examples of applied decoration. There is no longer a universal language of symbolism, and the gropings of some critics towards the imposition of 'meaning' on what they call post-modern architecture has been fairly unfruitful.

This apparent vacuum can in fact easily be filled. There is a latent national interest in decoration. You only have to look at the thriving DIY industry! Long-lasting traditions of ornament go back to our Celtic forebears, and a glance into any ancient parish church can reveal amazing decorative secrets.

'A bare outline won't do; give us the details.'

*M*any people think that a revival of classicism can help. It is certainly a universal language but it is not one that can be applied easily unless it is thoroughly learned. It is not the simple pastiche that some critics claim it to be: learning the classical language of architecture does not mean that you only produce endless neo-Georgian-style houses. Classicism provides an incredibly rich inventory of infinite variety.

*I*n Britain there has always been a parallel stream of the Gothic and the Arts and Crafts movements. These rich traditions rest in the hands of skilled craftsmen whose rare talents need constant nurturing to ensure their continuation. They are there, so why don't we use them more often?

*W*e need to reinstate architecture as the mistress of the arts and the crafts. I would suggest that the consumers are ahead of the professionals here. They seem to feel, as I do, that living in a factory-made world is not enough. Beauty is made by the unique partnership of hand, brain and eye. The results should be part of all new architecture, helping it to enrich our spirits.

St George's Hall, Liverpool

ART

While decoration is concerned with repetition and pattern, a work of art is unique. Why is it that contemporary artists play such a small part in the creation of our surroundings? Architects and artists used to work together naturally; today they are worlds apart. Look at so many of the great buildings of the past, where the architect needed the contribution of the artists to complete the splendour of his total vision. Imagine London's Banqueting House in Whitehall without Rubens' great ceiling; or the Sheldonian Theatre in Oxford without its sculpted emperors.

Quadriga facing Constitution Hill, London.

Rubens' great ceiling in London's Banqueting House.

Warner cinema, Leicester Square, London.

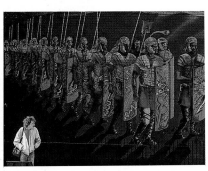

A mural painted adjacent to an old Roman wall in Manchester.

'Michelangelo accepted very few commissions for a free-standing abstract sculpture in the forecourt.'

How dull, in comparison, are some of our recent national landmarks. No artists were commissioned to adorn the National Theatre, which does not even boast a statue of our most famous playwright. Where is the art on the plans for the British Library? Architects and artists should be betrothed at an early stage in any major public project. It is no use just standing a sculpture on a plinth outside a new building, almost as a guilty afterthought. Art should always be an organic and integral part of all great new buildings. Sculpture and painting play an essential role in conferring on public buildings their unique social and symbolic identity, which architecture alone cannot. Their pictorial iconography is an essential complement to the architecture. Much more art should be commissioned.

It will be hard for this unity to come about satisfactorily as things are at the moment. Artists and architects might as well be educated on different planets. The principles by which art and architecture are taught need to be revised. There should be common disciplines taught to all those engaged in the visual arts. Life drawing and a study of nature is as essential for architects as it is for any artist. Remembering common roots can nourish both these great arts for their mutual benefit and our delight.

Above: Bludgeoning corporate imagery of the worst kind.

Above: A figure in armour heralds an 'historical town', but the town itself is hidden by the road signs.

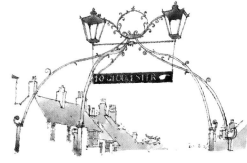

Above: A rare and quiet approach.

Above: Good lettering must be taught and learnt.

Above: Lights that are a pleasure to look at even during the day, unlike the avenue of ugly modern sodium lights (left).

— S I G N S & L I G H T S —

Thornbury, Avon

*F*ar too many of the marks of 20th-century progress take the form of ugly advertising and inappropriate street lighting, apparently designed only for the motor car. The car and commerce are both vital to the well-being of the country, but it is the junk they trail with them that we have to tackle.

*M*uch of commerce and retailing seems to have a strange affection for banal logos, and the result is that the country is littered with a proliferation of corporate images. These images may give the companies concerned a clear identity, but they can be crude and damaging in our older towns and in the landscape. The decline of the elegant shopfront with good lettering and its replacement by standard plastic signs is much to be regretted. There is something demoralising about great companies making so little effort to respect the places where, after all, their customers live. We could learn from some of our European neighbours about controlling signs, particularly within historic towns.

**'Don't make rude signs
in public places.'**

Michelin Building, London

The Michelin Building in London makes a virtue out of the desire to advertise. Below left: It is more usual nowadays for corporate imagery to be at odds with the buildings it is attached to. Below right: The old Elliott & Sons shop in Westbourne Grove was as large, but far more sensitive.

*T*raffic signs and street lighting are aspects of the visual world that need to be kept under control. On the great national motorway network as well as on British Rail and the London Underground there has to be constant vigilance about visual standards, especially the quality of lettering. Good lettering must be taught and learned; its qualities are timeless and classical in the broadest sense.

*S*treet lamps and lighting on the main traffic routes are often excessive and cast an alien sodium glow over large areas of the country. In parts of Britain there is no longer any real darkness or twilight, only an orange glare seeming to indicate a fire. Our towns and villages should be beautifully lit at night. Safety is not a matter of light intensity but of the overall quality of the surroundings. Many great cities of the world have retained a magic quality at night due to incandescent lighting. We should bury as many wires as possible and remember that when it comes to lighting and signs the standard solution is never enough.

COMMUNITY

Village Hall, Shernborne, Norfolk

*P*eople should be involved willingly from the beginning in the improvement of their own surroundings. You cannot force anyone to take part in the planning process. Legislation tries to make it possible for people to share some of the complex processes of planning, but participation cannot be imposed: it has to start from the bottom up.

*T*he right sort of surroundings can create a good community spirit. Too many areas of our towns and cities have suffered from the mentality of planners who zoned everything, keeping work and home miles apart and encouraging commuting. Good communities are usually small enough for people to get together to organise the things they want. This is possible in the inner cities as well as in smaller towns and villages.

*P*ride in your community can only be generated if you have some say in how it looks or how it is managed. The use of local builders, craftsmen and architects helps to achieve this.

*T*here is a great need for more experiment in the management of community development. The

Above: Isledon Road Community Plan, Finsbury Park. Locals lobby at Islington Town Hall. Left: Two residents of John Darling Mall at Eastleigh enjoy a chat. Architect Colin Stansfield Smith.

Below: Residents of Beechwood Lodge, Hampshire, a new home for the homeless designed by Edward Cullinan (right).

'Let the people who will have to live with what you build help guide your hand.'

professionals need to consult the users of their buildings more closely. The inhabitants have the local knowledge: they must not be despised. People are not there to be planned for; they are to be worked with. In the creation of new communities the problems may be more difficult, but there is always local knowledge and that is where a community starts.

*I*t is time for more experiment in the way we plan, build and own our communities. For example, new initiatives are needed to try and find ways to ensure that our surroundings are not entirely sacrificed to the car.

*I*n other areas sharing is a good way to start. The fine facilities of so many local authority schools and colleges, for example, could have a much wider community use. Churches could have an extra role as part of the healing process, working with doctors and hospitals. Schools and universities could, at certain times, be open to people of all ages.

*A*ll these things are part of a broader interpretation of 'planning' and 'community'. There must be one golden rule — we all need to be involved together — planning and architecture are much too important to be left to the professionals.

I hope these ground rules may provide a return to our roots and an enlightened view of the way ahead. Only when we've cleared away the undergrowth of worthless rules and dogma can beautiful architecture flourish again in the Kingdom.

It is not only sites of historic importance that need to be scrutinised by the public. Just around almost every corner there are places like St Andrew's Mansions. This is a block of 19th-century flats near Baker Street in London. There is a pleasant courtyard with rather unexpected terraces and galleries. Other than that, it's fairly typical – not especially remarkable, but much loved by those who live in it.

A developer put in an application to build an extra storey. It's not exactly Paternoster Square, but the residents feared it would cut out the sunlight and alter the whole face of the building. They felt passionate and were prepared to get together and do something about it. Strong feelings alone don't win planning appeals. The residents lobbied councillors, and steeped themselves in our seemingly unfathomable planning regulations.

Left: St Andrew's Mansions, a late-Victorian block of flats near Baker Street in London. Places like this give character and charm to a city.

Anna Sanders, Secretary of the Residents' Association, said, 'Fighting the present planning regulations is a complete nightmare really, because as soon as you've fought off one application and you've rallied all the support and made all your objections and got all your neighbours and local groups to write, the developer puts in another one, and your previous objections don't count, so you have to start all over again. It's been a very hard year and it's been a lot of pressure for all the residents here, and quite frankly we can't wait for it to be over.'

The application to develop St Andrew's Mansions was eventually heard by the Planning Committee of Westminster Council. One of the councillors pointed out that it was, after all, in a conservation area, and the application was refused on a majority decision.

Above: I recently went to St Andrew's Mansions to celebrate the residents' victory with them. Right: Summer 1988, when they were preparing for battle.

Y̶ou don't have to brief counsel to fight a planning case. Such as they are, the planning regulations are instruments of democracy: they are there to be used. And, whatever the shortcomings of the planning system, it is there for our benefit. We need to learn to use it. After all, it was determined conservation groups who drove back the juggernaut of 60s planning, not the professionals.

I am sometimes accused of wanting to return to the past, to encourage everyone to live in a kind of glorified Disneyland. That is not the case at all. But I do believe that if we are going to come up with an architecture we might actually take pleasure in, we have to strip away some of the nonsensical dogma of the day and think about fundamental principles once again.

Above: Malham Dale in Yorkshire:
limestone country. Man has made his
mark on this landscape, with the
materials which were to hand.

I do like architecture which respects nature. I find it hard to appreciate architecture which shouts at you that it is in competition with nature, an architecture which emphasises the rational element in our humanity to the exclusion of the intuitive. Hence the strictly utilitarian designs of the modern movement: flat roofs, uncompromising angles, an absence of any decoration at all, the love affair with revolutionary artificial building materials which so often prove unsatisfactory in the end.

I am sure that many people admire the wonderful landscapes we have in this country – particular parts of Derbyshire or the Yorkshire Dales, for instance, where the countryside is criss-crossed by stone walls. Now if those walls were built to the same dimensions in breeze blocks, for example, then I suggest the self-same walls would become eyesores. A similar thing would happen, funnily enough, if they were built of brick in that particular environment.

The trick, it seems to me, is to find ways of enhancing the natural environment, of adding to the sum of human delight by appreciating that man is more, *much* more, than a mere mechanical object whose sole aim is to produce money. Man is a far more complex creation. Above all, he has a soul, and the soul is irrational, unfathomable, mysterious.

In most cultures, rich decoration is as natural on accompaniment to the act of worship as music. Above: Wall paintings in a chapel at Longthorpe Tower in Cambridgeshire. Left: A richly ornamented dome in Samarkand. Right: Valldemossa, a village in Majorca where Frederic Chopin had a house and which I sketched a few years ago, is the result of building in sympathy and harmony with the environment. Even the terraces on the hillsides seem almost sculpted by the hand of some sympathetic artist.

'What shall it profit a man, if he shall gain the whole world and lose his own soul...?' Left: Widnes, Cheshire. Under the layers of modern life, a nagging sense that man has a soul. Below: 'I do like architecture which respects nature...' The temple at Sounion, Greece: the classical tradition with God, Man and Nature in equilibrium. The evolution of the Greek column and the classical orders was the result of a search for perfection rather than originality. The rules of proportion were the key to the creation of beauty, which the Greeks saw as a sacred act.

Ever since man began to build, he has acknowledged this vital aspect of himself, whether through some form of pagan worship which led him to want to decorate and embellish his buildings, or through a desire to glorify God and to build in sympathy and harmony with God's creation on this earth.

Throughout history, our ancestors have derived their inspiration from the infinite richness of the natural world. Architecture ever since the Greeks has witnessed a succession of revivals and ideas gleaned from the past. Our age is the first to have seen fit to abandon the past, or to deny its relevance and the lessons learnt over thousands of years. It is the first to have despised the principles of

mathematical harmony and proportion and to have embarked on a course which glorifies the triumph of science and man's domination over nature.

From trees to buildings

All Western architectural traditions have taken inspiration from nature. The Neo-classicists of the eighteenth century admired the simplicity of the forest. The Gothic Revivalists of the nineteenth admired nature's sheer abundance. All the Romantics were fascinated by the sacred in nature. It is only in more recent times that architects have seen fit to celebrate the achievements of man, rather than those of God, in their works.

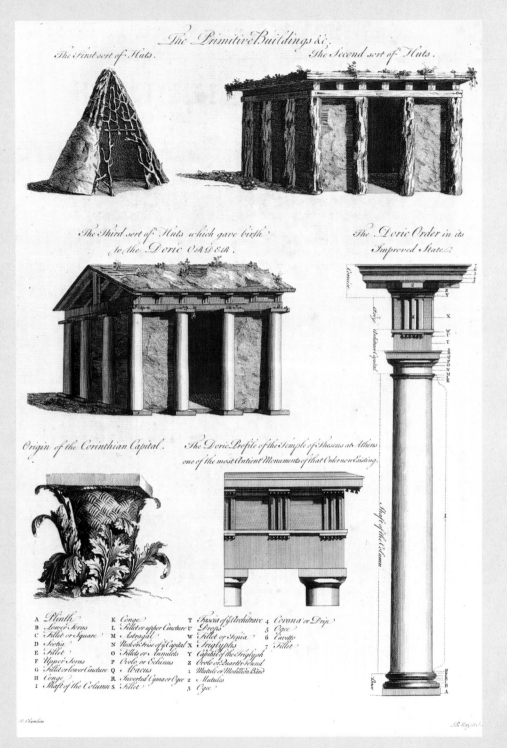

The Primitive Buildings &c.

The First sort of Huts.

The Second sort of Huts.

The Third sort of Huts which gave birth to the Doric ORDER.

The Doric Order in its Improved State.

Origin of the Corinthian Capital.

The Doric Profile of the Temple of Theseus at Athens one of the most Antient Monuments of that Order now Existing.

John Ruskin, who inspired the Oxford Museum (1855, detail of capitals, below), encouraged craftsmen to express their affection for nature and the world around them through the work of their hands.

Eighteenth-century theory linked the classical orders to origins in nature. William Chambers (above, far left), traced the evolution of classicism in his Treatise on Civil Architecture (plate of 1791, left) – which grew out of his architectural lessons to King George III.

Chateaubriand, the French Romantic, wrote that 'Forests were the first temples of God.' Above: The vaults in the cloister of Gloucester Cathedral are reminiscent of the branches of some great forest. Few architects seem willing nowadays to look to nature for inspiration. In New York Roger Ferri (his Hypostyle Hall, below) takes his cue from plants, the human figure, and from his fascination with the 'geometry of the universe'.

All this coincides with what can only be described as the denial of God's place in the scheme of things and the substitution of man's infallibility. The result, I would suggest, has been a profound dis-ease amongst countless people who are forced to live in the kind of surroundings sired by this unbalanced attitude. It's sometimes just as well to remind ourselves that nature still exists and so do architectural traditions that can suggest alternatives to what is generally on offer today.

It's always intrigued me as to how Greek temples originated and why it is that columns became such an important element in Greek buildings. I was recently rummaging through the Royal Library at Windsor and came across a book by Sir William Chambers who was architectural tutor to King George III in the days when Royal personages actually had architectural tutors (every now and then it's recommended that *I* should have some instruction in architecture as well…!)

A royal tradition

I have long been fascinated by an earlier Prince of Wales, Prince Henry (above), elder brother of King Charles I. He was a great patron of art and architecture. It was he who first appointed Inigo Jones (who revived classical architecture in this country), as Surveyor. Tragically, the Prince died when he was eighteen. It was said that 'if God had prolonged his dayes, he had caused build many curious and sumptuous buildings.' Below: The Queen's House at Greenwich, by Inigo Jones, was commissioned in 1616 by Anne of Denmark, Consort of King James I and mother of Prince Henry. It must have seemed revolutionary at the time because it looked back to antiquity and broke away from the Gothic past.

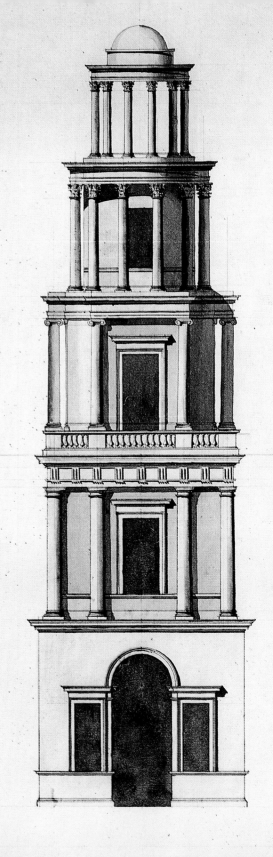

Left: King George III was an accomplished amateur draughtsman. Under his drawing master he produced elegiac watercolours of classical ruins in the landscape (above). His architectural tutor, William Chambers, taught him to produce vivid studies of neo-classical buildings. Drawing this tower (facing page) allowed the King to demonstrate his knowledge of the Orders of classical architecture.

He makes an interesting point which rather bears out my feelings, which is that such primitive buildings did begin using tree trunks as columns which developed gradually into the various orders of architecture.

From then on such columns when arranged in a harmonious order by an architect have given a mysterious sense of well-being and a kind of contentment to successive generations of human beings who still have that primeval relationship with trees lodged in their subconscious.

Some people believe that a return to classical principles now would solve our architectural problems. That's not quite the point. It's not only a question of style. What we really need to do is to regain the humility to understand the lessons of the past: not just of classical architecture, but of Gothic and other traditions as well.

At Highgrove, my home in Gloucestershire, I've been working with a local craftsman, adding some classical ornament and detail to the house.

In addition to the changes to my house at Highgrove (right), I have recently taken an interest in the design of a new residential wing at Kensington Palace (above and left). I wanted it to respect the contributions of previous architects who worked at the Palace and it has been named 'Hawksmoor House' after one of them. I suggested to the architect that a clock tower might be appropriate and, to my amazement, he agreed!

Of course, there was a time when the Prince of Wales could build on a rather grander scale. The Prince Regent worked with architect John Nash to enlarge the Pavilion at Brighton in the early 19th century. The extraordinary interior was damaged by the Great Storm of 1987, and I went down to Brighton to see how the restoration work was going.

It was intriguing for me to see what one of my predecessors got up to. The Pavilion has ornament and decoration in abundance that wouldn't be out of place in a film of the Arabian Nights, designed and executed in the spirit of carnival. Of course, this kind of thing would not be appropriate everywhere. But modernist 20th-century architects wanted to abolish such things as historical reference, and some thought 'ornament' was a crime. To deny such ebullient extravagance is, to my mind, a shame.

Above: The recently restored Music Room of the Brighton Pavilion. It started out as a fairly simple holiday home for the Prince Regent (left), but under the direction of architect John Nash it became the gloriously oriental extravaganza you see on the right.

Many of my ancestors showed a great interest in architecture. Prince Albert was an avid reader of the *Builder*. He involved himself deeply in the provision of more modest housing by collaborating on the designs for a 'Model House for the Working Man' for the Great Exhibition. It was re-erected and still stands in a park in Kennington. All around it lies land owned by the Duchy of Cornwall.

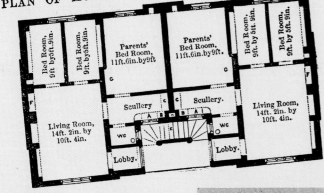

PLAN OF MODEL HOUSES FOR FOUR FAMILIES.

Bed Room, 9ft. by5ft.9in.

Bed Room, 9ft.by5ft.9in.

Parents' Bed Room, 11ft.6in.by9ft

Parents' Bed Room, 11ft.6in.by9ft.

Bed Room, 9ft. by 5ft. 9in.

Bed Room, 9ft. by 5ft. 9in.

Scullery.

Scullery.

Living Room, 14ft. 2in. by 10ft. 4in.

Living Room, 14ft. 2in. by 10ft. 4in.

Lobby.

Lobby.

SCALE OF

REFEREN

A, Sink, with coal-box under.
B, Plate-rack, over entrance to dust-shaft, D.
C, Meat-safe, ventilated through hollow bricks.

the catalogue
be more useful
ficulties these
were ready on
h the shilling
part of their
contains a de-
. Digby Wyatt,
tory matter.

USE, IN THE

and House was
nsen and Gerard
have been the
S. note by Inigo
io," in Worcester
was 162 feet in
square. All that
see is the curious
rmounted by the
he front originally
al letters instead of

, of plain Italian
dsome portal leads,
at you stand in the
excited city. The
he Lion, inscribed
above the façade (an
alone enable you to
e back are grass, gra-
ng trees. The stair-
It has a central flight
anches right and left;
olu railing and lamps,
arved marble podium.
house, however, is the
rtment of large size,
hly) ornamented with
boys, and foliage fully
series of fine copies of
Athens, Marriage of
others. Amongst the
the walls of the other
l be found choice speci-
tian, Vandyke, Salvator,
ers. Admission till now
h difficulty.

CONDUCTORS.

s number, in the account
Assembly Hall struck by
serve that "the spire had

these occurrences re-
ould imagine their cost to
ment: but from having

MODEL HOUSES FOR FOUR FAMILIES ERECTED AT THE CAVALRY BARRACKS, HYDE-PARK.

His Royal Highness Prince Albert, as President of the Society for Improving the Condition of the Labouring Classes, has had this building raised with a desire of conveying practical information calculated to promote the much needed improvement of the dwellings of the working classes, and also of stimulating visitors to the Great Exhibition whose position and circumstances may enable them by the carrying out of similar undertakings to benefit those who are greatly dependent on others for their home and domestic comforts.

In its *general arrangement*, the building is adapted for the occupation of four families of the class of manufacturing and mechanical operatives, who usually reside in towns, or in their immediate vicinity; and as the value of land, which leads to the economising of space, by the placing of more than one family under the same roof, in some cases, renders the addition of a third, and even of a fourth story desirable, the plan has been suited to such an arrangement without any other alteration than the requisite increase in the strength of the

is made in each
The water-closet is fitted up with a
shire glazed basin, which is complete without
any wood fittings, and supplied with water
from a slate cistern in common of 160 gallons,
placed on the roof over the party and staircase walls. The same pipes which carry away
the rain-water from the roof serve for the use
of the closets.

CONSTRUCTIVE ARRANGEMENT.

The peculiarities of the building in this respect are, the exclusive use of hollow bricks for the walls and partitions (excepting the foundations which are of ordinary brickwork), and

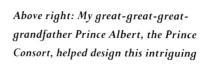

Above right: My great-great-great-grandfather Prince Albert, the Prince Consort, helped design this intriguing

'model house' (above left) for the Great Exhibition of 1851. As you can see, I have a precedent to follow.

Woodstock Court is a particularly fine example of sheltered housing, as we now call it, completed in 1914. I was fascinated to discover that my great-grandfather, King George V, when Prince of Wales, took the lead in social reform by reconstructing some of the slums of Lambeth as a model estate, to be an example to other landlords.

Nearby is Newquay House. It contained exemplary flats when first built by the Duchy in the 30s, but is in need of attention now. My great-uncle, King Edward VIII, took an interest in the design of Newquay House. The Duchy of Cornwall has now sold it to a housing association, but before that happened I asked the architect Ben Derbyshire to think about what to do first with the large block and to find out what the tenants wanted. An interesting dialogue ensued between architect and tenants, and it was suggested that some of the tenants might like to visit another similar scheme in Richmond, to see what could be done.

Above: Woodstock Court with Newquay House behind it. Right: Meeting some of the residents of Newquay House.

The architects Adshead and Ramsey were renowned pioneers of 'planning' in this country. They created a civilised architecture employing the simplest of means. The houses in Courtenay Square (above and left) of around 1914 are not of the finest materials, nor richly decorated, nor on a grand scale. The Square works because of its proportions and straightforward detailing. John Simpson's designs for the Duchy's Pentire Crescent in Newquay, Cornwall (right) will, I hope, succeed for the same reasons.

Another example in this area is Courtenay Square – a subtle reinterpretation of a Regency square, carried out in a 'progressive spirit', to use King George V's own description. The aim was to have as few flats and as many houses as possible.

The Duchy of Cornwall is a large land holding, mostly scattered around the West Country. As Duke of Cornwall I have the chance to influence a certain amount of building here. The Duchy has to be run as an efficient business. And, of course, it has environmental responsibilities in some of England's most beautiful countryside.

The Scilly Isles, also part of the Duchy of Cornwall, are picturesque, traditional and economically fragile. It's against this background that important decisions have to be made.

A developer came to the local council with proposals to build an hotel on St Martin's, one of the more isolated islands. An hotel would bring employment and money to the islands – which at the same time badly need more room for visitors. The Duchy considered the views of local people. Some of them would have preferred everything to remain as it was.

Some felt that the proposed site was in a very attractive part of the island which is extremely sensitive environmentally, and that, however carefully designed, the hotel was bound to detract from the lovely landscape and the natural beauty of St Martin's. But we ensured that it would be tucked out of sight of the island itself. And I have taken considerable trouble to see that it will be a good-looking building and that it will fit into the local surroundings.

Left: Eastern Isles and St Martin's, Scilly Isles.

So, having seen the proposals at the drawing stage, I asked that the hotel should be built more in the style of the local fishermen's cottages; that the materials should be traditional stone and slate; and that the roof-line should be broken up, not monotonous. I also think, quite strongly, that window surrounds should be in white, not always that voguish 'stain' colour.

I do believe that architectural 'adventurousness', producing non-traditional 'exciting' buildings, is certainly inappropriate in rural areas. It is essential, it seems to me, to have definite local rules about building. I recently went to Brittany which is similar in many respects to the Scilly Isles and found out that such rules are precisely what they have there.

Above: Hugh Town, St Mary's, Scilly Isles. Bold and supposedly 'imaginative' schemes here would look particularly grotesque.

Below: The new hotel on St Martin's will be traditional in style and as unobtrusive as possible.

London's Royal Free Hospital looks like an office block. It is doubtless superbly efficient medically, but body and soul shrink when confronted with menacing architecture such as this.

I have a feeling that there is a sincere desire now for buildings, and their settings and layout, which will raise our spirits once again and give us joy by their scale and by the attention to every detail. Such attention to detail and to human scale creates that elusive quality of *character*, and every nationality has a subtle way of expressing it differently.

Such a change of emphasis and the realisation of where we have gone astray may hopefully lead us to look again at such questions as the design of hospitals, for example. I believe that it is most certainly possible to design features which are positively healing in such buildings. I feel sure that courtyards, colonnades and running water, for example, are healing features. It can't be easy to be healed in a soulless concrete box with characterless windows, inhospitable corridors and purely functional wards. The spirit needs healing as well as the body.

Right: Lambeth Community Care Centre by Edward Cullinan. The homely scale here and the interplay of light and shade must surely enhance the healing process. Mammoth hospitals, built like dreary office blocks on a devastatingly functional basis, depress the spirits, however good the health care.

Above: Trouble has been taken with the design of this staircase, and the decorative banisters provide interest and visual pleasure inside Dorchester Hospital.

Right: Pitched roofs, attractive brickwork and balconies give the hospital a domestic character. How much more welcoming than a stained concrete bunker!

By now you might be forgiven for thinking that I only like the architecture of the past, but I do like some of the good new buildings going up now. Things are getting better than they were, largely because people have made their own preferences clear.

A new hospital in Dorchester which I opened recently, designed by the Percy Thomas Partnership, seems to me to be on the right lines. Traditional materials are certainly used, but modern ones too. Anyway, it's interesting and attractive for patients and visitors, although rather an excessive amount of red paint seems to have been spilt on it!

Opposite Sir Edwin Lutyens' Cenotaph, in a most sensitive site in London's Whitehall, is a new Government building. It's traditional-looking, made with traditional materials, and it's an office block. At the back, an attempt has been made to reflect Norman Shaw's Old Scotland Yard. The architect is William Whitfield.

The new residential wing of the Royal College of Agriculture at Cirencester looks very attractive to me. It's by David Lea. To match the Cotswold style they reopened a local quarry to obtain the slates for the roof. There are, I suppose, hundreds of similar quarries that have been closed and they could be given a chance to provide the materials for new building.

Above: There is a nostalgic, Elizabethan feel to this eye-catching new Government office in Whitehall, and the architect has understood the need to harmonise with neighbours. Left: Why not a 'hat' on the top of the services tower? Right: Hooray for the local vernacular at Cirencester!

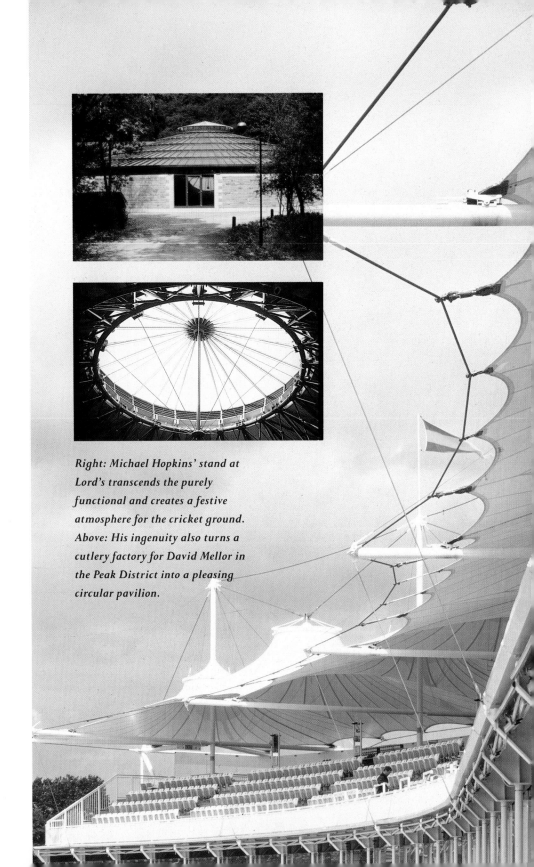

Above: Rolfe Judd & Partners' new offices in Cornhill. It's good to see windows with character, which don't give you a deformed reflection of yourself as you pass by, which so many fashionable glass buildings seem to do. Left: Skidmore, Owings and Merrill's Broadwalk House in Broadgate is of terra-cotta-coloured concrete and it provides quite a neat solution to the problem of designing a building at the apex of a triangular site. The tower resembles the spine of a half-opened book.

Right: Michael Hopkins' stand at Lord's transcends the purely functional and creates a festive atmosphere for the cricket ground. Above: His ingenuity also turns a cutlery factory for David Mellor in the Peak District into a pleasing circular pavilion.

Above: An imaginative use of brick and stucco, and references to older London styles, give these houses in Marylebone by Jeremy Dixon a welcoming intimacy. The rather eccentric windows add a distinct character to the whole street.

In the City a new office building which respects the scale and traditional materials of the old Square Mile – 68 Cornhill – is faced in stone and yet it looks modern. It's designed by Rolfe Judd & Partners.

In London's Isle of Dogs there is some good new housing. I very much like the Dutch-looking houses there designed by Jeremy Dixon.

You can't get anywhere much more traditional than Lord's Cricket Ground. But they commissioned Michael Hopkins, one of our most innovative architects, to design the new stand. It seems to me to catch the spirit of Lord's, giving a suggestion of marquee tents and Edwardian summer days. There are high-tech elements, with new materials blending in with the old.

Left: These striped crow-stepped gables and white bow windows are inspired in Jeremy Dixon's London Docklands housing.

Left: Terry Farrell's solid, classically chiselled Royal Regatta HQ at Henley adds considerable distinction to the banks of the Thames. A pity the centre couldn't be more substantial.

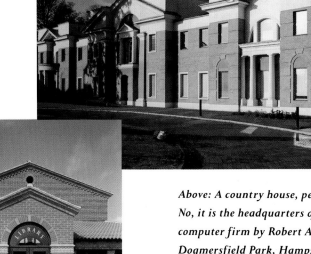

Left: At long last! John Outram has been brave enough, on the Isle of Dogs, to design a pumping station which soars beyond functionalism and enters the world of witty and amusing symbolism. Was it designed for passing Egyptian tourists to enjoy?

Above: A country house, perhaps? No, it is the headquarters of a computer firm by Robert Adam at Dogmersfield Park, Hampshire. The blank windows are a little disappointing, but the building shows that modern commercial life can thrive inside a shell that reflects a human scale and is at home in the landscape. Left: Robert Adam also designed this simple classical library at Bordon, Hampshire – the bricklayers enjoyed extending their talents here too.

Top left: Hillingdon Civic Centre by RMJM caused a stir, I seem to remember, when it was first built because it pioneered the departure from the nuclear-fallout-shelter look for public buildings. It is encouraging because it is made of brick and actually has pitched roofs.
Below and detail centre left: Is this new development at Richmond by Quinlan Terry merely pastiche? It may look familiar and have an 18th-century feel to it, but it is not just a series of copies of buildings from the past. The architect has used a familiar language to create an expression of harmony and proportion.

This is a personal choice of contemporary buildings. I don't expect everyone to agree with my choice but I like these buildings because their designers had the humility to recognise the value of their own architectural heritage. They have not sought to be egotistically 'modern' or 'revolutionary'. You will not find the fool's gold of the 'International Style', which has spread over so much of our world, represented here.

Top and above: The banks of the Severn in Shrewsbury are definitely enhanced by this new housing by Arrol and Snell. Old values of symmetry and geometry give the façade distinction, and the courtyard has privacy and elegance. Right: The exterior of the sheltered housing scheme in Towcester, Northamptonshire by Siddell Gibson sensibly echoes the appealing elements of one of this country's best legacies from the past: the almshouse. Such buildings were never grand, but always homely and, like many of the residents, displayed character and experience.

Above: The courtyard of this sheltered housing scheme in Wadhurst, East Sussex, also by Siddell Gibson, shows some encouragingly imaginative touches and picks up hints of local, traditional styles and materials. The sensitive design of the ventilators on the roof adds interest and provides the building with its individuality. Have you noticed how unfinished so many new housing developments seem nowadays without chimneys?

Above: For me the design of this building by Keith Critchlow, the Krishnamurti Centre, shows a special kind of flair and vivacity. The treatment of the roof-line and the dormer windows is inspired and, as far as I am concerned, gives the building an irresistible tactile quality. The chimneys are fun too, and their bevelled appearance produces splendid shadows. Left: The interior is equally stylish. Look at the *originality of the fireplace and how complementary it is to the perpendicular arches of the ceiling. The arches themselves, and the octagonal window above the door, provide the most soothing kind of decoration. None of it is pastiche, but it uses well-tried forms in a contemporary idiom.*

Right: These two houses in Suffolk, designed by Stephen Mattick, show that it is still possible to build really beautifully in the old traditional manner with exquisite brickwork and fine detailing. The great thing is that they are traditional-looking; that they might have been there for a few hundred years; and that they fit snugly, comfortably and reassuringly into the countryside. Above left: Canterbury Cathedral precincts, of all places, demand care and sensitivity. Architects Maguire and Murray show both these qualities in their new additions to the King's School. Bottom left: This irresistible construction wearing an 'Inspector Clouseau' thatch hat is a studio designed by David Lea. Traditional materials and techniques give great aesthetic pleasure: and it only cost two thousand pounds.

Far left: Frank Roberts' church in Preston is unusually sympathetic and reassuring. It is a relief to see a new church when so many are being sold to the highest bidder. And it is not made of concrete with trendy girders, instead the unusual buttresses (detail, left) enfold the doorway in a welcoming niche. Below: Roberts has unleashed his imagination with this exuberant, slightly Tibetan-looking, new stand at Towcester racecourse. Again it shows character and humour while fitting in with the site.

Left: Prince's Square, Glasgow. A welcome return of craftsmanship and the art nouveau traditions of turn-of-the-century Glasgow. While I was there I spoke to Alan Dawson, the craftsman responsible for the ironwork. Iron to him is an 'amazing material', he told me. He found it almost impossible to draw out fully

the designs for the iron railings at Prince's Square. He much prefers, he says, 'to take the bar itself, get it hot and shape it, and do the drawing with the material itself... sketching with iron.' How many of these skills have we wantonly thrown away by driving decoration and embellishment out of our buildings?

Another place I liked the look of was in Glasgow. We *can* have architecture with a sense of history. Prince's Square in Glasgow is a new shopping centre. Architect George MacKeith has designed a 'retail environment' that really does lift the spirits; it builds on tradition and reinterprets it. The inspiration of natural forms has certainly been acknowledged, and the skills of traditional craftsmen have been rediscovered. Stonemasons, carpenters and ironsmiths have all had a chance to demonstrate their art.

Glasgow is changing fast. After visiting Prince's Square I took the opportunity of walking around the old Victorian centre. It's true the Victorians themselves welcomed change with enthusiasm, and they knocked down the medieval city during *their* building boom

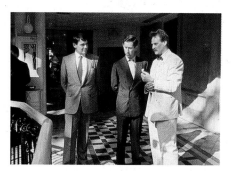

which I think was a great tragedy and our loss. But what they put in its place shows that an economic boom can inspire handsome buildings.

Above: Glasgow City Chambers (W. Young, 1883–88): putting Victorian prosperity to work by building magnificent public buildings and spaces.

More than any city in Britain, Glasgow retained its Victorian business centre. Not very long ago, the Victorians were mocked for their love of decoration. Nowadays we have learnt to look with some envy at their exuberance: the detail, the riot of styles, the unabashed use of ornament.

It is enthralling to look up at the roof-line, at its variety: to see how it avoids the deadening monotony of so many modern city skylines. But that wasn't just 'laissez-faire' exuberance. Victorian Glasgow didn't just happen. Merchants, conscious of their civic responsibilities, working within a great classical tradition, erected buildings which preserved grand but uniform frontages.

And they were prepared to put some of the wealth they created towards great public buildings. For example, the City Chambers are a testimony to civic self-assurance at a time when people still believed in celebrating the virtues of public life.

Above: Templeton's Factory made carpets and was inspired by the Venetian Gothic of the Doge's Palace. Above right: Stirling's Library: a classical interior where books are cherished, and the pursuit of knowledge given dignity by the architecture. Background: The Clydesdale Bank of 1873. Nouveau riche Victorian bankers who liked to see themselves as heirs to the merchants of Renaissance Italy, naturally enough chose a dignified classical style to invest their own transactions with importance and timelessness.

However, beyond Glasgow's centre the story is less happy. Thousands and thousands of people are condemned to live in dreary high-rise blocks. Parts of the old Gorbals were swept away to build such flats. The notorious tenements were not as bleak as their reputation suggested, but they had been neglected from the beginning of the 1920s. Nothing was spent on them by their private landlords. The tenements came to symbolise an old order which had no place among the Utopian visions of the post-war world.

Now the age of the bulldozer is over. The surviving tenements in Glasgow are being refurbished and are making attractive homes. But this change of heart didn't come without a fight from the local community.

Left: The Gorbals: a reputation for squalor led to the threat of total demolition. Right: The refurbished Gorbals. Saved by community action.

Before refurbishment and after. Below: The Gorbals revived: not just accommodation but part of Glasgow's character reborn.

John Butterly, Chairman of Reidvale Tenants' Association, explained, 'We were told by the council at one time back in the early 70s that they'd be starting at one end of this area with a bulldozer and stopping at the other end. We put up a fight against that and I think we've proven now that we were right. A lot of time, a lot of work, but we finally got there and I think the proof of the pudding, as they say, is about us.'

Right: The Red Road flats, into which hundreds of Glaswegians were moved after the destruction of their old communities, have the doubtful honour of being the tallest flats in Europe.

Above: A drawing lesson at the Glasgow School of Art in 1900 appears to have been a pretty decorous affair. But drawing was then fundamental to art – and architecture. Left: The library at Glasgow School of Art, a masterpiece by Charles Rennie Mackintosh, who respected natural forms, traditional materials, and the Scottish vernacular.

Opposite page: 'Drawing makes you look at the world…' This wonderfully skilful drawing for Somerset House is by Sir William Chambers.

In the course of this book we've seen many promising signs that things are on the mend. Community architecture and consultation has indeed helped people to have some say. But how did we go so woefully astray twenty years ago?

One answer is that leading modern architects not only persuaded the public to abandon the past, but also totally outlawed the teaching of traditional styles of architecture.

To this day, even at Glasgow's School of Art, where plaster casts line the corridors, you cannot learn classical architecture; nor can you anywhere else in Britain, for that matter. But at the School of Art, of which I have recently been asked to be Visitor, they at least continue to teach measured drawing when most other schools have abandoned it. That isn't just a convenient skill. It's fundamental.

Plan & flank
of the door —

N.B. the pilasters A to pr...
to receive the impost of

Above: Buildings on the Balmoral estate. Left: Drawing, I was glad to see, is firmly on the curriculum of this Glasgow primary school.

Drawing makes you *look* at the world, to visualise clearly what you see and what you propose to design. No amount of computers can substitute for that. I feel that if architects are not thoroughly versed in an architectural tradition, Gothic or Classical, no amount of community consultation can produce really good buildings.

Just as only recently it seemed archaic and pointless for students of architecture to learn to draw, so it was thought unnecessary to teach children to do so. We tended to over-emphasise self-expression. That, mercifully, is changing too. Some primary schools now pride themselves on teaching children really to look at what they're drawing.

In Britain we are sometimes accused of being 'visually illiterate'. Of course we're not, but we do now need a far greater emphasis on art and design and drawing skills in our schools, so that they are regarded as important, not 'weak', subjects. You can't start teaching children to draw too soon. If we *are* a nation that lost its ability to 'see', then we paid a terrible price for it.

Too many of our modern buildings are huge, blank and impersonal. We have created somewhat godforsaken cities from which nature, or indeed the spiritual side of life, has almost been erased. We don't *have* to build towns and cities we don't want, in which we feel manipulated and threatened by the architecture.

Not so long ago we had an agreed way of doing things, an unspoken code, if you like. Now, perhaps, we really need to write a few things down in a code. I'm not talking about the arbitrary and unfathomable regulations that already exist, which need a whole branch of the legal profession to interpret. I'm talking about a sort of 'ten commandments', or 'ten principles', with sensible and widely-agreed rules, saying what people can and what they cannot do.

Left: El Wakil's marvellous drawing for a vault, which he designed for a mosque in Jeddah. It expresses what is called 'sacred geometry', a subject which he is painfully relearning today from ancient Islamic building traditions.

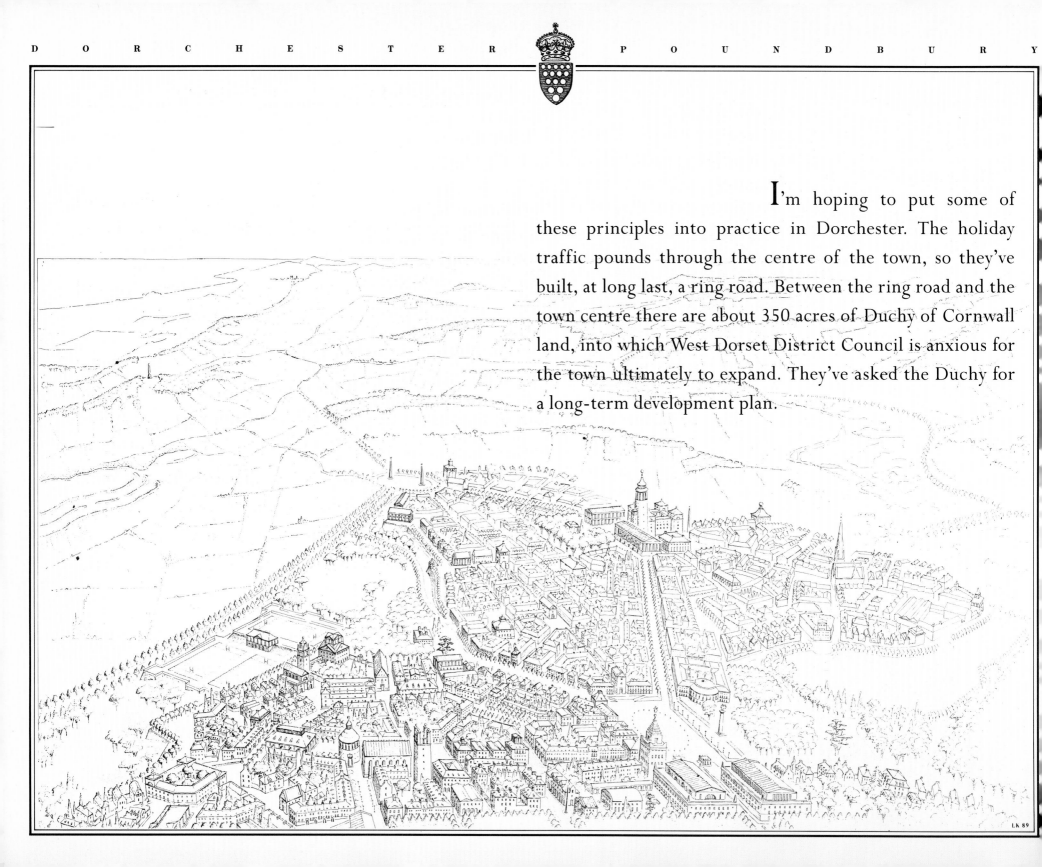

I'm hoping to put some of these principles into practice in Dorchester. The holiday traffic pounds through the centre of the town, so they've built, at long last, a ring road. Between the ring road and the town centre there are about 350 acres of Duchy of Cornwall land, into which West Dorset District Council is anxious for the town ultimately to expand. They've asked the Duchy for a long-term development plan.

Left: Leon Krier is brilliant at setting down a vision for a town or city. This is a preliminary sketch of what development to the east of Dorchester might look like. Obviously the participation of the people of Dorchester is needed, and hard economic calculations have to be made, before any building can start, but vision and boldness are also needed if we are to produce something of real beauty in the English countryside.

Above: A visit to Dorchester by The Prince of Wales in 1887. Below left: Owlpen, Gloucestershire: the epitome of the English village. Its character evolved through the slow passage of centuries of rural life. Below right: Lower Earley, Berkshire. An instant village: handy for the motorway and the superstore.

The easiest thing for the Duchy would have been to sell the land and leave others to do the development. But I am very keen to try something different. This is a problem facing the whole of southern England – how to build in our countryside without spoiling it.

Of course, the traditional English village shows how building can actually enhance the countryside. There are innumerable villages near my home in Gloucestershire which show what I mean. They are built of wood, slate and stone. They exploit the skills of craftsmen. They are designed to be a part of the landscape – but they developed in an organic, piecemeal way over hundreds of years. We haven't got that sort of time. But you *can* plan a village.

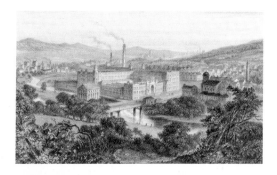

Top: Saltaire: Sir Titus Salt, a Nonconformist millionaire, made his fortune from alpaca. Round his factory near Bradford he laid out houses, a park, chapels, a library, and an Institute – but no public houses. Right: John Simpson's plan for the village of Upper Donnington in Berkshire: an attempt to create a living community, not just another housing estate.

Above: John Nash's Blaise Hamlet was the forerunner, in the early nineteenth century, of the picturesque English suburb. A few cottages carefully arranged around the village green.

Designing model villages has a long tradition – it goes back centuries. In the 19th century people were inspired to design industrial communities like Saltaire, near Skipton, and suburban developments like Bedford Park in London. Lord Leverhulme's vision and consideration created the remarkable Port Sunlight village to house his own employees in Birkenhead. And Britain pioneered Garden Cities like Letchworth and Hampstead Garden Suburb.

I was interested in the rather imaginative plans for Upper Donnington in Berkshire. It's not for me to say whether or not they've got it right for their site, but I can see that they are concerned with creating a community rather than merely building a housing estate, and they try to make use of the lie of the land.

Above left: Letchworth in Hertfordshire was the first of the pioneering Garden Cities. Inspired by Ebenezer Howard's book To-morrow: a Peaceful Path to Real Reform *(1898), which was written in reaction to the horrors of the industrial cities of the nineteenth century, Letchworth was an attempt to build an ideal community from scratch in the English countryside.*

Above: Bedford Park in west London grew up in the 1870s and 80s on the newly completed District Line, which made it possible to work in the City and live in supposedly park-like rural surroundings. Built in a Queen Anne style sometimes called 'Wrenaissance', it was much favoured by members of the middle class with artistic and cultural leanings.

Left: '…An extraordinary place.' Seaside, Florida is being built to a Code. Can it influence the future development of our cities? Top: Seafront pavilions which give a slightly eerie sense of occasion to a trip to the beach. Above: Seaside's neo-classical post office. Some people claim that classicism is the American style. Right: One of Seaside's gazebos. The Code encourages fantasy and imagination.

This kind of down-to-earth planning influenced cities around the world. I'm intrigued that these ideas – which seem to have lost their appeal here – can still be put to work elsewhere. On the Gulf of Mexico in America is a fascinating new development called Seaside. It's an extraordinary place – with a modern, classical look. Seaside is *planned*. And it's beginning to influence architectural thinking all over the United States.

The architects are trying to create at Seaside a community with the traditional virtues of the American small town and suburb. But the influence of the planned English garden city movement is strong. The developer and his architects devised the Code which lays down the materials you can build with. The Code stipulates how far apart the houses should be. Not far – neighbourly proximity is encouraged. The Code lists the colours you can paint your house. But the Code is much in favour of individual imagination – hence the town is full of towers, follies and gazebos. They believe that with the Code anyone can design his own house here – you don't have to be an architect.

The owner, Robert Davis, cuts a somewhat unusual figure for a developer. He's challenged most of the urban design thinking of the time and made a commercial success of building to the highest standards. As he explains, 'The idea of a neo-classical town is that it has pedestrian scale which obviously gets people out of their automobiles and uses up a great deal less petroleum. In addition to that there are limits to a town like this: it should have boundaries or edges beyond which there should be open space. That's one of the really essential things about traditional town planning, something which up until recently was considered fairly sacred in England as well.'

One customer is the architect and influential theorist, Leon Krier, who lives in England. He helped plan Seaside and designed his own house there. He has also designed a campanile, an exercise in neo-classical architecture which, one day, will give focus and form to the centre of Seaside.

Above: The house that Leon Krier built for himself at Seaside. Below: 'Atlantis', Krier's project for a planned city in the Canary Islands. It's based on the timeless canons of classical taste, and echoes some of the ancient Hellenistic cities, the ruins of which one can still see today in Greece and Turkey.

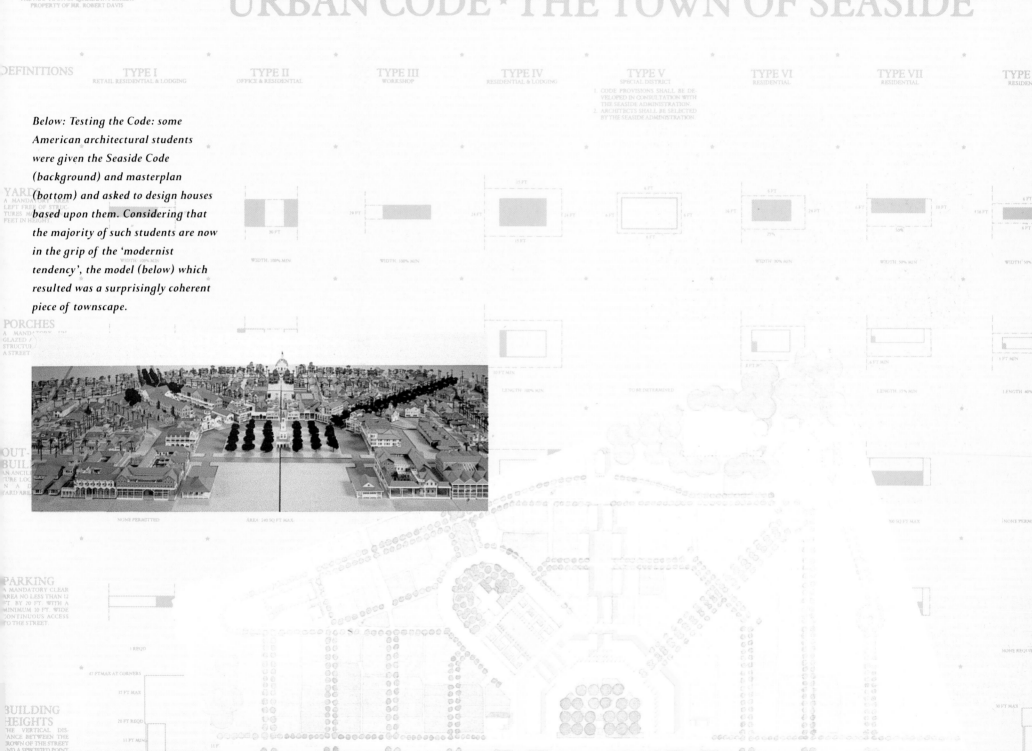

DEFINITIONS TYPE I RETAIL RESIDENTIAL & LODGING TYPE II OFFICE & RESIDENTIAL TYPE III WORKSHOP TYPE IV RESIDENTIAL & LODGING TYPE V SPECIAL DISTRICT TYPE VI RESIDENTIAL TYPE VII RESIDENTIAL TYPE V RESIDENTIAL

TYPE V — SPECIAL DISTRICT
1. CODE PROVISIONS SHALL BE DE-
VELOPED IN CONSULTATION WITH
THE SEASIDE ADMINISTRATION.
2. ARCHITECTS SHALL BE SELECTED
BY THE SEASIDE ADMINISTRATION.

*Below: Testing the Code: some
American architectural students
were given the Seaside Code
(background) and masterplan
(bottom) and asked to design houses
based upon them. Considering that
the majority of such students are now
in the grip of the 'modernist
tendency', the model (below) which
resulted was a surprisingly coherent
piece of townscape.*

YARDS
A MANDATORY...
LEFT FREE OF STRUC-
TURES...
FEET IN HEIGHT

PORCHES
A MANDATORY...
GLAZED...
STRUCTURE...
A STREET

OUT-
BUILDINGS
AN ANCILLARY
STRUCTURE LOC...
IN A...
YARD AREA

PARKING
A MANDATORY CLEAR
AREA NO LESS THAN 12
FT BY 20 FT WITH A
MINIMUM 10 FT WIDE
CONTINUOUS ACCESS
TO THE STREET

BUILDING
HEIGHTS
THE VERTICAL DIS-
TANCE BETWEEN THE
CROWN OF THE STREET
AND A SPECIFIED POINT
IN A STRUCTURE

Top: A typical house in Seaside. Note the compulsory porch as an aid to communal living. Above: A non-typical house. The Code puts a characteristic stamp upon everything which is built at Seaside, including this house by a modern architect from New York.

One of the curiosities of the Code is that it says that porches (and all the houses must have one) should not be further than a few feet from the street, so that you can be within chatting distance of passers-by. And again, the picket fences have to be painted white, and made of wood. The Code is very much against artificial materials. As Robert Davis says, 'I think the picket fences look better as the paint starts to peel and the wood starts to split a little bit. It gets a patina whereas the alternative will never have a patina – it will only look worse…'

People will say 'It's all very well for those with money…' But I believe that the lessons they've worked out at Seaside have very serious applications both in rural areas and in our cities. The founders certainly believe that a sense of real community will grow here; that people will *live* here. I wish them well. But – even with sensible regulations – a sense of community is not easily achieved. Living together also requires an act of the spirit. And that is not easily found in the late 20th century.

It is commonplace to say that medieval cities like Siena in Italy are beautiful, that they are civilised. They are places we want to go to, rather than get out of. But such beauty was not inevitable. Siena was, and is, a banking city – once the most important in Italy – a city with a living to make. But its citizens believed in rules that expressed their ambition to live within harmonious and beautiful surroundings. Interestingly, Siena has always had a

Code. As Vittorio Mazzoni Della Stella, Siena's Mayor, explained, 'This town has had urban planning regulations for 700 years. The first record we know of relates to the form of windows and the distance between buildings – and that's from 1295. So for seven centuries the public authorities in Siena have regulated construction work and changes to the city.'

Left: Old stone streets still make enjoyable places for people to live and work in.

Top: The striped marble richness of the Cathedral and (left) the glorious fountain in the Campo both show the love and artistry lavished on the city of Siena.

Opposite page: The tiny town of Brolio in Tuscany is so carefully built that I had a hard job painting it as it almost disappears into the landscape.

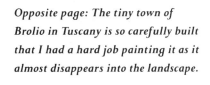

Left: The shops have to display their 'signage' with modesty and consideration for where they are; the signs are displayed within the architectural framework, not plastered all over it like so many of ours.

Of course, Siena was the result of more than just enlightened planning legislation. The city was born of a time when people believed that 'Except the Lord build the house, they labour in vain that build it.'

'The city is the image of the soul,' wrote St Catherine of Siena, 'the surrounding walls being the frontier between the outward and inward life. The gates are the faculties or senses connecting the life of the soul with the outward world. Living springs of water rise within it. And in the centre, where beats the heart, stands the holy sanctuary.'

But, of course, the 20th century came to Siena too. The usual rash of modern buildings began to spread round the outskirts, out of sympathy with the architecture and the materials of the old city. The Sienese saw the problem and sought a solution. They went back to the spirit of the old regulations from which a simplified Code was extracted. The emphasis was on conservation: new activities should be accommodated in old buildings.

Above: The Sienese have done business in buildings like this for centuries.

Left: In Siena every street leads to the Campo and life unfolds there like a theatrical spectacle. Traditionally the square is said to follow the shape of the cloak of the Virgin Mary, representing a safe haven at the heart of the city. For scale and harmony in town planning Siena has never been bettered.

Overleaf: Lorenzetti's 'Good and Bad Government' (1337–39) in the civic hall shows the city of Siena. For the first time in European art history the artist sees the well-planned city as an allegorical embodiment of higher spiritual values.

The Sienese respect their old buildings. I heard of no great movement to pull them down to make way for buildings 'appropriate' to the times. Siena was the first Italian city to pedestrianise. The centre of the city is where people *live*. The regulations make it difficult for commercial businesses to move in and take over. And tourists, though important, don't overwhelm it or distort the city's character.

But, for me, perhaps more significant than any of these things is the great central area of Siena – the Campo. The Campo was designed, so it is said, to suggest the protective cloak of the Virgin, lying spread across the heart of the city.

Those were the days. In our time it's a lucky city, especially in Britain, that doesn't have its heart torn out and thrown away. But it is *our* time. We *can* see reason again if we really want to.

VOLGIETE GLIOCCHI A RIMIRAR COSTEI VOI CHE REGGIETE CHE QVI FIGVRATA 7 PSVA CELLĒCA CORONATA LAQVAL SĒPRA CI

I would like to emphasise above all else that the views I have about architecture, about design and about their relationship to the natural environment of which we are such an integral part, are my own personal views. I do not expect everyone to agree with my opinions. But, if some people feel they are in sympathy with them, then obviously I am delighted. My chief object has been to try and create discussion about the design of the built environment; to rekindle an alert awareness of our surroundings; inspire a desire to observe; and, most importantly, challenge the fashionable theories of a professional establishment which has made the layman feel he has no legitimate opinions.

Everywhere I go, I get a very strong impression that most people know the sort of buildings they like. They are buildings that have grown out of our architectural tradition and that are in harmony with nature. These were the qualities that made our towns and cities such beautiful and civilised places in the past and, with God's help and inspiration, they can do so again.

C. 1986
KELSO

Left: A watercolour sketch by me of Kelso in Scotland. Background: A scroll from Batty Langley's 1745 pattern book for builders and workmen. Above right: New urns on the skyline at Richmond Riverside.

For those readers who may happen to be professional architects I dare say my expressed views have merely confirmed the opinions of those critics who say that since I have no professional training in architecture I should not be voicing my views so publicly. (The trouble with that particular criticism is that if you develop it logically you will find it precludes most politicians from expressing their views on most subjects.) I can almost guarantee I will also be told that my apparent preference for a more classical, some would say nostalgic, style in architecture is stifling 'modern creativity'. I will be accused yet again of living in the past; as if it were an abominable sin to respect, admire, cherish or seek inspiration from the richness of our heritage.

It was Edmund Burke who wrote that a healthy civilisation exists with three relationships intact. It has a relationship with the present, a relationship with the future, and a relationship with the past. When the past feeds and sustains the present and the future you have a civilised society. It was only in this century that we broke that pact with the past and tried to obliterate its meanings and its messages.

Architecture has always looked backwards ever since the time of the Greeks. The Romans discovered Athenian architecture. The Renaissance was based on a rediscovery of the Classical and Byzantine world. The 18th century also went back to Greece and Rome, and the English vernacular profited immeasurably from the incorporation of motifs which had their origins in the ancient world. Many an English market town – like Blandford or King's Lynn – has little details on its buildings that echo the work of Borromini and Bernini, the great Italian architects of the Renaissance. In the 19th century Greece, Rome and Byzantium, and many other places besides, were seen as perfectly reasonable sources for modern buildings. The great men of the engineering age such as Brunel and Paxton used classical, Gothic, even Egyptian, detail in their triumphantly technological buildings.

Nowadays, with the virtual demise of classical education and of any attempt to provide schoolchildren with a perspective on our shared heritage of European civilisation, I suppose it is little wonder that any reference in our buildings to that European heritage is considered old-fashioned and irrelevant to today's 'modern' conditions. What is worse, such reference is dismissed derisively as 'pastiche'. The very word suggests that an ability to learn from the past is uncreative and deadening. It is inevitably used as an insult, accompanied by wearisome references to 'Disneyland'.

In fact, a respect for the past both disciplines and liberates at the same time. It gives us a measure for our own achievements as well as an endlessly rich source of examples for us to use.

The skills, the crafts, the art that went into the architecture of the past are still there – just. But they need to be revived and put to work again, so that we can build cities, towns and villages which seem to have grown out of the historical fabric of Britain and which better reflect the true aspirations of its people. We must concentrate on creating environments in which people can prosper psychologically, as human beings, not merely as cogs in a mechanical process. We need design and layout which positively encourage neighbourliness, intimacy and, where possible, a sense of shared belonging to a recognisable community.

What is the point, for example,

of being the most technologically advanced society if, at the same time, we lose our soul, and forfeit the right to be considered civilised? For this is what we have allowed to happen by deluding ourselves that we are somehow immortal; by losing our faith in eternity; by believing that this Earth was made for our dominion, and by losing that proper sense of humility which enables us to live in gentle harmony with our surroundings and with God's creation. Why else is it that we now find ourselves confronted by such complex and disturbing environmental problems threatening, as they do, the very survival of this planet and *all* its living inhabitants?

Everything cries out for a reappraisal of our values and attitudes. Don't be intimidated by those who deride such views. They have had their day. Look at the soulless mess in which they have left us all…! Look at what has been done to the developing countries in the name of progress and technology. We have managed, through our Western arrogance, to make at least two generations feel ashamed of their ancient, traditional customs, culture and spiritual values. Now, I suggest, is the time when we should, in all humility, learn from our Third

World neighbours. Perhaps they can teach us, before it is too late, how to reacquire those eternal values which, if properly understood, and blended with our technological expertise, could provide us with the essential balance and sense of proportion that we need in order to sustain both the visible and invisible aspects of our world.

You may ask how all this is relevant to what some people derisively term my 'pet hobby horse' – architecture? The answer is that since I believe architecture has always been the outward expression of an inner inspiration, it is only too clear that it has become dangerously unbalanced and, unless it is examined in the light of a reappraisal of basic values and principles, we will all be the poorer. I just pray that this book will provoke some thought and reflection on a subject which will affect, not only ourselves, but also our descendants yet unborn.

Right: Bow, 1988.

A Vision of Britain was transmitted on 28th October 1988 on BBC1's Omnibus programme. I am grateful to the entire BBC team, particularly Nicholas Rossiter, the director, John Daly, the cameraman and Jeff Shaw, the film editor, all of whose professionalism and tact I came to take for granted. My personal and special thanks go to Christopher Martin, the producer, who, somewhat to my surprise, persuaded me to make a film about architecture and who then saw it through to the end.

I would like to thank **John Sergeant** and **John Nankivell** for their fine illustrations, created specially for this book.

Photographs reproduced by gracious permission of Her Majesty The Queen are as follows: from the Royal Collection, pages 56, 57, 108 (top left), 109 (bottom) and 111 (bottom left); from the Royal Library, Windsor, pages 106 (middle), 108 (right) and 109 (top).
Photographs on pages 110 (right), 116 (bottom) and 138 are reproduced by permission of the Duchy of Cornwall.

Acknowledgement is due to the following for permission to reproduce photographs and illustrations:
Adlib Picture Library 88 (top, middle and bottom left) photos David Evans;
ARCAID 120 (background) photo Richard Bryant;
Architects' Journal, 1956 69 (bottom);
Associated Design Consultants 23 (left), 24 (top and bottom left), 29 (left), 32 (top and bottom left), 33 (bottom), 34 (left), 39 (middle), 43 (left), 45 (bottom), 46 (top and bottom left), 47, 49, 53 (top), 56 and 57 (overlay), 59 (bottom left), 69 (top and middle), 85 (top), 87, 93 (top), 94 (bottom left, centre middle and bottom), 95 (bottom left), 113 (top), 114 (top and bottom left), 117, 120, 139 (right);
Ed Barber 21 (bottom)
Oliver Benn 110 (top and bottom left);
John Bethell Photography 78 (top left), 84 (bottom right), 103 (top and bottom left), 107 (top), 108 (bottom left);
City of Birmingham Handbook, 1950 34 (top right);
Birmingham Post 34 (bottom right);
Bow Neighbourhood Centre 39 (top), 156;
Bridgeman Art Library 42, 45 (top), 50 (right), 68, 93 (upper middle);
Bristol Museum and Art Gallery 140 (bottom left);
British Broadcasting Corporation 23 (right), 35 (middle), 39 (bottom), 41 (bottom), 43 (right), 46 (right), 54 (right), 65 (bottom), 71 (right), 100 (inset), 101 (right), 105 (right), 115 (right), 129 (right), 133 (top), 134 (right), 136 (bottom), 147 (right), 149 (bottom);
British Library 64 (left), 65 (top);
Steven Brooke Studios, Miami 142, 143, 144 (top), 145 (inset bottom), 146 (top);
James Brotherhood & Associates 24 (right);
Richard Bryant 15;
John Burgee Architects 60 (bottom);
Geremy Butler Photography 135;
Camera Press 7 (left);

Cannon Bridge Developments Ltd 63 (top left);
Cardiff Bay Development Corporation 31 (bottom);
J. Allan Cash 14 (middle);
Chapman Taylor Partners 35 (bottom);
Martin Charles 97 (top), 118 (top), 126 (top left);
Peter Cook 119 (bottom right);
County Hall Development Group 44 (right);
Country Life 127 (left and top right) photo André Goulancourt;
Crampin & Pring 28 (left), early artist's impression;
Detheridge Ltd 31 (top);
John Donat 66 (right);
Duany/Plater-Zyberk 145 (full page and inset middle);
El-Wakil Associates 12 (top) drawing Edwin Venn, (bottom) photo A.W. El-Wakil, 137 drawing Edwin Venn;
England Scene 18 (top left), 30 (right), 35 (top), 44 (middle left), 53 (full page), 149 (middle left);
Mary Evans Picture Library 14 (left), 112 (middle and right), 139 (top left), 141;
Farmer Design Group 29 (right);
Terry Farrell & Co 44 (bottom left and background), 63 (bottom left and right);
Mark Fiennes 119 (top and bottom left), 123 (middle and bottom);
Fine Art Photographic Library 50 (left), 51, 74;
John Freeman 18 (bottom left), 19 (right), 38, 64 (right), 84 (top left), 147 (left), 151;
Stephen Garnett 25;
City of Glasgow 131 (right), 132 (right), 133 (middle and bottom);
Glasgow School of Art 134 (top) photo Annan & Sons Ltd, 134 (bottom left);
Tim Graham Picture Library 136 (middle);
Greater London Photograph Library 21, 36 (top left, middle and top and bottom right), 37 (left), 44 (top left), 58 (bottom left), 66 (left);
Sonia Halliday 105 (left) photo F.H.C. Birch;
Hampshire County Architect's Department 96 (bottom left) photo Joe Low;
Robert Harding Picture Library 115 (left);
Harrison Greenwell Partnership 33 (top);
Lady Harrod 79 (bottom);
Scott A. Hedge 146 (bottom);
Nick Hedges 40;
Hulton Picture Company 132 (left);
Hunt Thompson Associates 96 (top left), 113 (bottom);
Hunting Aerofilms 16, 86 (top left), 104;
Anwar Hussein 11;
Imperial War Museum 58 (top left);
Tim Imrie 126 (right);
Leon Krier 144 (bottom);
Landscape Only 18 (middle), 19 (left);
Carl Laubin 73 (top), 121 (bottom);
Leeds City Council 26, 27, 28 (top left and top and middle right);
London Regeneration Consortium 62;
Magnum Photos 10 photo Peter Marlow, 93 (bottom) photo Ian Berry;
Prakash Maisuria 8, 9, 89 (middle);
Mansell Collection 112 (left);
Hugh Martin Partnership 128, 129 (left and middle);
D.H. Mayhew 89 (bottom);
MetroCentre 79 (left);

Mitchell Library, Glasgow 130, 131 (left and background);
Museum of London, Museum in Docklands Project 52, 58 (bottom right);
Museum of Modern Art, New York 107 (bottom);
John Nankivell 78 (bottom left), 81, 83 (bottom), 90 and 91 (background), 92 (bottom left), 95 (background);
Network 36 (middle left) photo Mike Abrahams;
Newcastle Initiative 13 (left) photo Mike Blenkinsop;
Olympia and York 54 (top and bottom left);
Paternoster Consortium 70, 71 (top and bottom left), 72 (top and bottom left);
Photo Source 83 (middle) photo A. Williams, 86 (bottom right) photo E. Nagele;
Press Association 7 (right);
Jo Reid and John Peck 121 (top);
Rex Features 13 (right), 14 (right);
Francis B. Roberts 127 (bottom right);
Royal Academy of Arts 106 (left), 107 (background);
Royal Pavilion, Art Gallery and Museums, Brighton 111 (top, centre and right);
St Martin's Properties 48;
Salt Estates Ltd 140 (top);
SAVE Britain's Heritage 67 (left and right);
Philip Sayer 20;
SCALA 149 (top and middle), 152–3;
Schofield Shopping Centre 28 (left);
Scottish Development Agency 133 (right);
Mike Seaborne 53 (middle);
John Sergeant 78 (right), 82 (top), 84 (top right), 86 (top right), 88 (right), 90 (top right), 92 (top right), 94 (right), 96 (right);
John Simpson & Partners 72 (right) photo ADP, 73 (bottom), 114 (right), 140 (right);
Speciality Shops 28 (bottom right);
Stirling, Wilford and Associates 67 (right);
Tony Stone Worldwide 18 (top right) photo Tom Ang, 60 (top) photo Dave Saunders, 60 (middle), 102 photo Colin Raw, 139 (bottom left) photo Rob Talbot;
Jessica Strang 79 (middle), 80 (top, middle and bottom left), 83 (top), 84 (bottom left and middle), 86 (bottom left), 89 (top), 93 (lower middle), 94 (top and middle left and top centre), 95 (right);
Swansea City Council 30 (left);
Tate Gallery 55 (right);
Telegraph Colour Library 18 (bottom right) photo R. Hallman, 150;
Quinlan Terry 155 (top centre) photo Mark Fiennes;
Thomas Photos, Oxford 92 (bottom right);
Percy Thomas Partnership 118 (bottom left) photo Jeremy Cockayne;
Times Newspapers 59 (top and middle left);
Tower Hamlets 41 (top);
John Twinning 37 (top, middle and bottom right);
Weidenfeld & Nicolson archive 106 (right);
Emma Williams 99, 100 (background), 101 (left);
Philip Wolmuth 97 (bottom);
ZEFA 59 (right) photo K. Kerth, 117.

Watercolours and sketches by the author appear on the following pages:
6, 17, 22, 61, 103 (right), 136 (top), 148 and 154.

Figures in italics refer to captions.

Abingdon, Oxfordshire (Town Hall)
   80
Adam, Robert *122*
Adelaide House, London 47
Adshead and Ramsey *114*
aesthetics 11, 15, 79
air-conditioning systems 77
air-rights building *62*
Albert, Prince Consort 112, *112*
almshouses 87, *124*
aluminium 88
Anne of Denmark *108*
Architectural Association 77
architectural schools 12, 13
Arrol and Snell *124*
art 92–3
art and design 136
art deco *63*
art nouveau *129*
Arts and Crafts movement 91
Arup Associates *71*, 72, *72*
Athenian architecture 155
Atkins, Madge 39, *39*
'Atlantis' project *144*

Balmoral *7, 136*
Banqueting House, Whitehall,
   London 92, *93*
Barber, Mrs Robin *8*
Bath 85; The Circus *84*
BBC (British Broadcasting
   Corporation) *8*, 9, 65, *65*
beauty 15, 43, *43*, 63, *64*, 77, *78*, 91,
   105, 139
Bedford Park, London 140, *141*
Beechwood Lodge, Hampshire 97
Belcher, J. and J. 66
Belfast City Hospital *8*
Bernini, Gianlorenzo 155
Birkenhead 140
Birmingham 33, *34, 35*, 77; Bull
   Ring *34, 35*, 35; Central
   Library, Paradise Circus *32*;
   International Convention
   Centre *33*; Mason College *32*
Blandford, Dorset 155
Blitz, the *58*
Bologna 14
Booker, Christopher 43
Bordon, Hampshire *122*
Borromini, Francesco 155
Bow, London 37, *39, 39*, 41; Albany
   Place 39
Bowen, Mr and Mrs J.E. *8*
Bradford, Yorkshire *140*

brick *18*, 37, 65, *73*, 88, 102, *118,
   121, 122, 123, 126*
Brighton Pavilion 111; Music Room
   111
British Library 65, 93; Reading
   Room *64*, 65
British Museum Reading Room
   64, 65
British Rail 95
Brittany 116
Broadwalk House, Broadgate,
   London *120*
Brodrick, Cuthbert *27, 28*
Brolio, Tuscany *149*
Brunel, Isambard Kingdom 155
brutalism *32*
Builder 112
building acts 82
Building Centre *8*
Building News 8
Burford, Oxfordshire 79
Burgee, John *48*
Burke, Edmund 155
Business in the Community 14
Butterly, John 133
bye-laws 82
Byzantium 155

Canaletto, Antonio 55, 58
Canary Islands *144*
Canary Wharf, London Docklands
   52, 53, 54, 55, 55
Cannon Street station, London *62*
Canterbury Cathedral 126
car parks *34*, 41
Cardiff 31; City Hall *30*
Cardiff Bay 31, *31*
cars, priority of 33, *34*, 79, *79,
   94*, 97
Cascades housing development,
   London Docklands *53*
Castle Combe, Wiltshire *84*
Cat Castle stone quarry, County
   Durham 89
Catherine of Siena, St *149*
Cenotaph, Whitehall, London 119
chain stores 25
Chambers, Sir William 44, 106, *107,
   109, 134*
Channel Tunnel *62*
character 17, 117
Charing Cross station, London *63*
Charles I, King *108*
Chateaubriand, François René,
   Vicomte de *107*

Chelmsley Estate, near Solihull, *37*
Cheltenham, Gloucestershire 85
Chesterton, G.K. 13
chimneys 50, *124*, 125
Chippenham, Wiltshire 80
Chopin, Frederic *103*
churches 81, 97, *127*
Cirencester (Royal College of
   Agriculture) *119, 119*
clapboarding 88
classical architecture *43*, 72, *72, 73,
   73*, 91, *105*, 109, *109*, 110, *122,
   134*, 143, *143*, 144, *144*, 155
cob 88, *88*
codes 13, 14, 15, 80, *137*, 143, *143,
   145, 146, 146, 147*, 149
Cole, George V. *43*
community 96–7, *140, 140*, 146, 156
community architecture movement
   13, 134
concrete *7, 32*, 33, 37, 39, *44*, 59,
   88, 117, *118, 120, 127*
Conisbrough Castle, South Yorkshire
   (Visitors' Centre) *8*
conservation 28, 149
conservation areas 66, *66*
conservation groups 101
Constable, John *45*
convention centres *32, 33*
Cornwall, Duchy of 112, 113, 114,
   114, 115, 138, 139
corporate imagery *94, 95*
Cotswold: stone *18*; style 119
County Hall, London *44*
craftsmen 11, *18*, 89, 91, 96, *129,
   129*, 139
Critchlow, Keith *82, 125*
Cullinan, Edward 97, *118*
Cumbernauld, Strathclyde 77

Dallas, Texas *60, 61*
Davis, Robert 144, 146
Dawson, Alan *129*
'Daytime Live' (television
   programme) *8*
decoration 11, 90–91, 92, *103*, 111,
   129, 130
Della Stella, Vittorio Mazzoni *147*
Derbyshire 78, 102
Derbyshire, Ben 113
developers/development 9, 15, 27,
   28, *35*, 53, 62, 63
Devon *88, 88*
Dixon, Charles Edward *50*
Dixon, Jeremy 121, *121*

Dogmersfield Park, Hampshire *122*
Dominion Monarch (ship) *52*
Dorchester, Dorset 138, *139*
Dorchester Hospital 118, *118*
Dorset 88
drawing 134, *134*, 136, *136*
Duany, Andres 14
Dutch style 121

Eastbourne, Sussex (DIY store) *8*
Eastern Isles, Scilly Isles *115*
Eastleigh (John Darling Mall) 96
Edinburgh 14, 85; New Town *14*
education 9, 12
Edward VII, King (as Prince of
   Wales) *139*
Edward VIII, King 113
Egyptian detail *47, 122*, 155
Elliott & Sons, Westbourne Grove,
   London 95
El-Wakil, Abdel Wahed 11, *12, 137*
enclosure 86–7
'Enterprise Zone' 53
Environment, Department of the 9
Evans and Shalev 15

farmhouses 82
Farnham, Surrey (Lion and Lamb
   Yard) *29*
Farrell, Terry 44, *63, 122*
Fathy, Dr Hassan 11
Fens 78, *78*
Ferri, Roger *107*
Festival of Britain *44*
Finsbury Park, London (Isledon
   Road Community Plan) 95
flint 88
forests 106, *107*
Foster, Norman *62*, 70
Fróxfield, Wiltshire (almshouses)
   86

garden cities 140, *141*, 143
Gendall, John *50*
geometry *107, 124*; sacred *137*
George III, King 106, *107*, 109
George IV, King (as Prince Regent)
   111, *111*
George V, King 113, 114
Gladdis, Catherine *8*
Glasgow *129*–34, *136*; City
   Chambers *130, 130*; Gorbals
   132, *132, 133*; Prince's Square
   129, 129; Red Road flats *133*;
   School of Art 134, *134*

glass 77, *120*
Gloucester Cathedral *83, 107*
Gloucestershire 139
Gosney, Ron 8
Gothic architecture *43*, 91, *108*,
   109, 155
Gothic Revival *32*, 48, 106
Great Exhibition (1851) 112, *112*
Great Fire of London 58, *58*
Great Storm (1987) 111
Greek architecture 76, 105, *105*,
   107, *144*, 155
green belts 79
Greenwich 55, *55*; Queen's House
   108
Greenwich Hospital 55
Guildford, Surrey (Friary shopping
   centre) *29*

Hackney, London 37
Hampstead Garden Suburb 140
harmony 69, 84–5, *103*, 123
Henley Royal Regatta HQ *122*
Henry, Prince of Wales *108*
Herefordshire 88
hierarchy 80–81
Highgrove, Gloucestershire 110,
   110
high-rise housing 43, 132; *see also*
   tower blocks
high technology 10, 121
highway regulations 15
Hillingdon Civic Centre *123*
Hind-March, Mrs S. *8*
Holford, Lord 69
Hopkins, Michael *120*, 121
hospitals 118, *118*
Houses of Parliament, London
   43, 43
housing associations 15, 23, 113
housing estates *7*, 12, *36*, 37, 87
Houston, Texas *61*
Howard, Ebenezer *141*
Huck, Mrs 23
Hugh Town, St Mary's, Scilly Isles
   116
Hydra, Greece *12*
Hypostyle Hall *107*

inner cities 12, 14, 96
international style 10, 77, 123
Islamic architecture 11, *11, 137*
Isle of Dogs, London 121, *122*
Islington, London 80; Town Hall 96
Isozaki, Arata 70

glass 77, *120*

James I, King *108*
Jeddah *137*
Jeddah Corniche *12*
Johnson, Philip *48*
Jones, Inigo *108*

Kelso, Scotland *155*
Kennington, London 112; Brandon
   Estate *21, 36*
Kensington Palace *110*
Kent 88
Kilpeck Church, Herefordshire *90*
King George V Dock, London
   Docklands *52*
King's Cross station, London *62*
King's Lynn 155
King's School, Canterbury *126*
Knott, Ralph 44
Krier, Leon *139*, 144, *144*
Krishnamurti Centre *82, 125*

Lambeth 113; Community Care
   Centre *118*
Lancaster, Osbert 79
Lanchester and Rickards 30
land, respect for 78–9
Langley, Batty 155
Laubin, Carl *73*
LCC Redevelopment Plan for
   London (1943) *36*
Le Corbusier 9, *37*
Lea, David 119, *126*
Leaderfoot, Scotland *19*
Leeds: Corn Exchange *28*; Kirkgate
   market, *27, 28*; Quarry Hill flats
   27; Town Hall *27*
Letchworth, Hertfordshire 140, *141*
lettering *94, 94*, 95
Leverhulme, Lord 140
lighting: incandescent 95; sodium
   79, *94*; street *94, 94*, 95
Lincolnshire 78
listed buildings 66, *67*
Liverpool (St George's Hall) 92
local planning authorities 89
London 58; Bedford Square 85;
   Cornhill *120, 121*; Courtenay
   Square 114, *114*; Gordon Place
   86; Marylebone *121*; Oxford
   Street 37; Paternoster Square
   69, *69*, 70, 71, 73; Poultry
   (No. 1) 10; Quadriga
   (Constitution Hill) *93*; St
   Andrew's Mansions, near Baker
   Street 99–100, *99, 100, 101*;

Westbourne Grove 95; Whitehall 119, *119*; *see also* individual buildings and districts
London Bridge City 48
London City Corporation 69
London Docklands 50, *50*, 52, 53, *53*, *121*; Canary Wharf *52*, 53, *54*, 55, *55*; Cascades housing development 53
London Underground 95
London Wall 63
Longthorpe Tower, Cambridgeshire *103*
Lord's Cricket Ground *120*, 121
Lorenzetti, Ambrogio *151*
Louvre, Paris *14*, 15
Lower Earley, Berkshire 87, *139*
Lower Slaughter, Gloucestershire *18*
Lund, N.M. 69
Lutyens, Sir Edwin 119

McCaughey, Paula 8
MacKeith, George 129
Mackintosh, Charles Rennie *134*
Maguire and Murray 126
Malham Dale, Yorkshire *102*
Manchester 93
Manhattan, New York 59, *61*
Mansion House, London 69, 71
Mappin & Webb 66, 66
markets 25, 27, *28*, 34
Marlborough, Wiltshire 84
Marx, Karl 65
materials: artificial 102, 146; local 10, 15, *18*, *19*, 188–9; revolutionary 7, 76, 102; traditional 11, 72, 116, 118, *124*; *see also* individual materials
Mattick, Stephen 126
Mellor, David 120
Metro Centre, near Newcastle 79
Michelangelo 93
Michelin Building, London 95
'Model House for the Working Man' 112, *112*
modernist architecture/modernism 9, 10, 11, 73, 81, *145*
Mondial House, London 46, *46*
Montparnasse, Paris 14
Montparnasse Tower, Paris *14*
Monument, the, London 46, 47
Morrison, Herbert 36

Napoleon Bonaparte *14*
Nash, John 111, *111*, *140*

National Gallery, London 7
National Theatre, London 44, 45, 93
National Westminster Bank Tower, London 47, 55
nature: harmony with 153; man's domination over 105; study of 93
neo-classical architecture *106*, *143*, 144
neo-Georgian architecture 73, 91
neo-vernacular style 23
New York 53; Battery Park City *54*
Newcastle *41*; Newcastle Theatre Village *13*; Urban Development Corporation 13
Newquay, Cornwall (Pentire Crescent) *114*
Newquay House, London 113, *113*
Northamptonshire 88
Northumberland 82
Notre Dame Cathedral, Paris 59, *59*
Nottingham: Victoria Flats *8*; Victoria Railway Station *8*
Nottinghamshire 82, 88

oast houses *18*
O'Connor, John 74
offices 33, 44, 47, 73, 77, 80, 119, *119*
Old Scotland Yard, London 119
order, sense of 10, *43*
ornament: at Brighton Pavilion 111; at Highgrove 110; and Victorians 130
Outram, John *122*
Owlpen, Gloucestershire *139*
Oxford: Museum *106*; Nuffield College 86; Sheldonian Theatre 92

Paris 14
'pastiche' 12, *25*, 73, 91, *123*, *125*, 155
Paternoster Square 69, *69*, 70, 71, 73
Paxton, Joseph 155
Pei, I.M. 15
Pelli, Cesar 54, 55, *55*
Percy Thomas Partnership 118
petrol stations 79
Pittsburgh 60
planning 9, 78, 97, *114*
planning appeals 99
planning legislation 77, 79, 96, 149

planning regulations 15, 53, 76, 79, 82, 99, 100, 101, 147
plaster *18*
plastic cladding 88, *89*
Port Sunlight village, Merseyside 140
Portsmouth (Tricorn Centre) *8*
post-modernist architecture 7, 10, 63, 90
power stations 79
Prague 14
Preston 127
proportion 105, *105*, *123*
public enquiries 76
Putney, London (Post Office Sorting Office) *8*

quarries 89, *89*, 119
Queen Anne style *141*

railway lands 62
Regency style 114
Reidvale Tenants' Association 133
Renaissance 10, 155
Richmond, Surrey 113, *123*, 155
Richmond, Yorkshire 86
RMJM *123*
Roberts, Frank 127
Roehampton, London 84
Rolfe Judd & Partners 120
Roman architecture 155
Romanticism 106
Ronan Point 37
roof-line 116, *125*, 130
roofs: flat 102; pitched *118*, *123*; tiled *18*
Roosevelt, Eleanor 41
Royal Academy, London 9
Royal College of Agriculture, Cirencester 119
Royal Free Hospital, London *117*
Royal Institute of British Architects (RIBA) 7, 9
Rubens, Peter Paul 92, *93*
Runcorn (Earl's Way) *10*
Ruskin, John 106

St Magnus Martyr, London 47
St Martin's, Scilly Isles 115, *115*, *116*
St Mary's, Scilly Isles *116*
St Pancras station, London 65, *81*
St Paul's Cathedral 46, *46*, 50, 55, *55*, 58, 59, 69, *69*, 70, 71, 72, 73, 86

Salisbury Cathedral *83*
Salt, Sir Titus *140*
Saltaire, near Skipton 140, *140*
Samarkand *103*
San Gimignano, Tuscany *61*
San Marco, Venice 59
Sanders, Anna 100
Sandringham House, Norfolk 15
sandstone *19*
Saudi Arabia 10
scale 14, *24*, 35, 69, 72, 78, 79, 82–3, 117, *118*
schools 9, 97, 136, *136*; architectural 12, 13
Scilly Isles 114–15, *115*
Scotland 7
Scottish Highlands *18*
Seaside, Florida 14, 143–4, *143*, *144*, 146, *146*
Seaside Code 143, *143*, 145, 146, *146*
Seine river 59
Severn river *124*
Shaw, Norman 119
Sheffield (Odeon Cinema) 89
sheltered housing 113, *124*
Shernborne, Norfolk (Village Hall) 96
shop signs *24*, *29*, 94, *149*
shopping centres 25, *29*
Shrewsbury, Salop 124
Siddell Gibson 124
Siena 14, *147*, 149, 151, *151*; Campo 86, 149, 151, *151*; Cathedral 149
signs: road 94; shop *24*, *29*, 94, *149*; traffic 95
Simpson, John 48, 72, 73, *114*, 140
Skidmore, Owings and Merrill 120
Skipton, Yorkshire 23, *23*; Craven Court 25, *25*; High Street *24*; Skipton Building Society *24*, 25
skyline 49, 55, 58, 59, *60*, 79, 82, 130
skyscrapers 58, 60
slate *18*, *19*, 23, 116, 119, 139
slum dwellings 36, 37, 113
Smirke, Robert 64
Smith, Colin Stansfield 96
Smith, Mrs M. *8*
Soho, London 37
SOM 44
Somerset House, London 44, *134*
Sounion, Greece *105*
Southwark, London 36

Spitalfields, London 37
Steele, James 11
Stepney, London *36*
Stirling, James 66, 70
stone 24, *73*, 88, 89, *89*, 102, 116, 121, *139*, *147*; Cotswold *18*; local 23, *23*; whitewashed *18*
Street, G.E. 84
stucco *121*
Suffolk 126
supermarkets 79
Sussex 88
Sutton (Hastoe) Housing Association 15
Swansea Docks 30
sweat shops 37
Swindon, Wiltshire (The Link Centre) *8*
Sydney 60
symmetry *124*

Taj Mahal *11*
technology 10, 11, 12, 54, 76, 77, 156; engineering *19*
tenements 132
terraced housing 13, *21*, 23
Terry, Quinlan *123*
Texas 55
Thackeray, W.M. 64
Thames river 44, 48, 50, *122*
thatch *18*, 88, *126*
Thaxted, Essex *82*
Third World 156
Thornbury, Avon 94
tiles *18*, 88
timber *18*, 88
To-morrow: a Peaceful Path to Real Reform (Howard) *141*
Toronto 53
Towcester, Northamptonshire *124*; racecourse 127
tower blocks *21*, 37, 39, *39*, *41*, 49, 53, 54, *54*, 55, *55*, 59, 67, *133*; *see also* high-rise housing
Tower Bridge 50
Tower Hotel, London *49*
Tower of London 49
town planning, traditional 144
traditional architecture 10, 73, 134
Treatise on Civil Architecture (Chambers) 106
Trentishoe, Devonshire *78*
Truro, Cornwall (Courts of Justice) 15, *15*
Turkey *144*

Turner, J.M.W. 55, *55*
Tweed river *19*
Twigg Brown 48

'Upon Westminster Bridge' (Wordsworth) 45, 49
Upper Donnington, Berkshire 140, *140*
'urban villages' 14

Valldemossa, Majorca *103*
Van der Rohe, Mies 66
Vancouver *61*
Venice 58
Vienna 14; Karl Marx Hof *27*
Vision of Britain, A (film) 9

Wadhurst, East Sussex *124*
Warner Cinema, Leicester Square, London 93
Waterloo Bridge 45
Wealden House, Sussex 88
Wensleydale, Yorkshire 23
West Dorset District Council 138
Westminster Bridge 45, 49
Westminster Council Planning Committee 100
Whale, Jim 25
Whitby, Yorkshire *19*
White City, London 65, *65*
Whitfield, William 119
Widnes, Cheshire *105*
Wilson, Professor Colin St John 64
windows *120*, 121; blank *122*; bow *121*; characterless 117; dormer *125*; frames 39; form of *147*; octagonal *125*; surrounds 116
Windsor Castle Royal Library 107
wood *139*, 146
Woodstock Court, London 113, *113*
Wootton Courtenay, Somerset *18*
Wordsworth, William 45, 49
'worker housing' *27*
Wren, Christopher 46, *47*, 55, 69, *73*
'Wrenaissance' *141*

Yorkshire Dales 23, 78, 102
Young, G. *130*